SACRED WISDOM

# THE TAO TE CHING

Lao Tzu

A New Translation,
Commentary and Introduction by

Ralph Alan Dale

BARNES & NOBLE BOOKS
NEW YORK

*The Tao Te Ching:* Translation, Commentary
and Introduction by Ralph Alan Dale
was first published in 2002
ISBN 1 84293 056 7

This edition published by Barnes & Noble, Inc.,
by arrangement with Duncan Baird Publishers,
Sixth Floor, Castle House, 75–76 Wells Street, London W1T 3QH

2005 Barnes & Noble Books

M 10 9 8 7 6 5 4 3 2 1

ISBN: 0 7607 6975 3



Library of Congress Cataloging in Publication data available

Typeset in Great Britain by Jerry Goldie Graphic Design
Printed and bound in Thailand by Imago

# INTRODUCTION

The *Tao Te Ching* is an ancient Chinese book composed of only five thousand characters and written perhaps as early as the sixth century BCE, by Lao Tzu, the legendary father of Taoism.

For centuries, this small book of Lao Tzu's sayings had no name. It was like the Tao itself that is introduced right at the outset:

> The Tao that can be told
> is not the universal Tao.
> The name that can be named
> is not the universal name.

More than four centuries after Lao Tzu was supposed to have lived, Si-Ma Qian (Ssu-Ma Ch'ien) observed that the book was divided into two parts. Thereafter people began to refer to these two parts as *Tao* and *Te*. Still later, the book was divided into eighty-one sections. Verses 1–37 are called the *Tao* section because Verse 1 begins with the word, *Tao*. Verses 38–81 are called the *Te* section because Verse 38 begins with the word *Te*. Then the word *Ching* was added to the title. *Ching* means *Ancient Text* or *Classic*.

Tao means *path*. For Lao Tzu, it signifies not just any path, but the specific path to living in concordance with the unity of the universe. According to Lao Tzu, it is the nature of nature to issue from an inextricable relationship of every part to the whole. To live life in accord with the Tao is to be in harmony with all others, with the environment and with one's self. It is to live in synchronicity with processes, and to be completely authentic, sincere, natural and innocent. The word *integrity* embraces all these characteristics. Tao also implies the inexhaustible greatness and wonderfulness of the universe and every part of it. All these propositions provide what modern science would call a theory of the nature of the universe. I therefore translate Tao as the *Theory of the Great Integrity*. Te means *virtue* or the practice of the Tao, and Ching, as already indicated above, means a *classic* book or *guide*. I therefore translate the *Tao Te Ching* as *A Guide to the Theory and Practice of the Great Integrity*.

The *Tao Te Ching* is one of the most widely translated books in the world. During the past 2,400 years there may have been as many as 1,400 different interpretations with perhaps 700 extant. This book continues to fascinate people throughout the world. Why?

I believe it is because the *Tao Te Ching* confronts and offers an alternative to our schizoid ways of thinking, feeling and behaving. Every section appeals to an innate holistic wisdom that our innermost being has longed for – sometimes consciously, often unconsciously – during all these past so-called civilized millennia. Lao Tzu's words invite us to transcend words, since words are used as the rationalizations of the tyrannies that we have established over each other. He offers us what in his time were alternative utopian pathways to a more harmonious life. Today, in this dawn of the twenty-first century, the Great Integrity presents itself as a practical and achievable goal and perhaps as the only alternative to our own species extinction.

Right at the beginning, Lao Tzu invites us to transcend words:

> In the infancy of the universe,
> there were no names.
> Naming fragments the mysteries of life
> into ten thousand things and
> their manifestations.

But how does one take issue with the world of words without using words? By being, rather than by arguing. That, in fact, was Lao Tzu's way. He probably never wrote this book because polemics was the very target of his advocacy. More likely, many generations of his disciples and followers summarized his philosophy of life in these metaphoric fragments which sing the literary music of the right brain, the transcendence of language through unordinary language.

Because paradox is the principal mode of Lao Tzu's thought processes, and because it is the nature of the Chinese language, especially ancient Chinese, to be poetic, I have rendered these 81 sections as verses, although the original is written more like Chinese prose than poetry. Moreover, how else than through poetry can one employ the left brain to transcend itself? How else can one criticize logical thinking without using logic? And how else does one merge yin and yang whose very nature expresses polarization?

Above all, it is not Lao Tzu's way to preach. He gently reminds us that preaching is a judgmental activity that negates the Great Integrity. But the very act of raising the flag of the Great Integrity is itself an act of preaching, one of the inherent paradoxes of the *Tao Te Ching*.

But the opposite of disputation and logic is not randomness and irrationality. I have attempted in these translations to preserve a subject focus while immersing each verse in the paradoxes that are at the heart of Lao Tzu's thought. The translations have deliberately avoided entrapment in either the prison of logic or in a hodge-podge of disconnected thoughts.

It is the paradox of every poet to have to transcend the logical function of language through language. It is a higher level of paradox when the very content of the poetry is dedicated to this transcendence. The ultimate consistency of Lao Tzu's wisdom is for us to communicate through silence, but consistency is also a negation of his wisdom. Since the *Tao Te Ching* itself is a communication through words, the very act of writing or reading this book is an affirmation that words are not really the enemy. The enemy is the perversion of words to manipulate the disadvantaged, and their further perversion to rationalize the consequent inhumanities of these manipulations. On the contrary, the words of Lao Tzu point us toward our liberation from inequities and injustices, that is, toward the Great Integrity.

What is the Tao? It is the oneness of all reality. According to Lao Tzu, the Tao or Great Integrity is the origin and nature of the universe. It is the way of life for all species on our planet, including human beings living in most tribal societies.

> In ancient times
> the people knew the Great Integrity
> in all its subtlety and profundity.

Later, since the advent of civilizations, we human beings lost the Great Integrity, exchanging our natural harmony with the universe for ego-oriented life styles. However, Lao Tzu expresses confidence that we will one day recover the Tao.

# *Verse 1*

## TRANSCENDING

The Tao that can be told
is not the universal Tao.
The name that can be named
is not the universal name.

In the infancy of the universe,
there were no names.
Naming fragments the mysteries of life
into ten thousand things
and their manifestations.

Yet mysteries and manifestations
spring from the same source:
the Great Integrity
which is the mystery within manifestation,
the manifestation within mystery,

the naming of the unnamed,
and the un-naming of the named.

When these interpenetrations
are in full attendance,
we will pass the gates of naming notions
in our journey toward transcendence.

## VERSE 1 COMMENTARY

We are not only reminded here that there is a dichotomy between the unnamed (our intuition) and the named (our reasoning), but also that these two seemingly opposite mind-worlds can be integral. Yet, *mysteries* (our intuition) and *manifestations* (our experience) spring from the same source: the universal Tao (the Great Integrity) by which Lao Tzu means the wholeness and holiness that is embedded in our nature and in the entire nature of nature. Lao Tzu also reminds us of the *mystery within manifestation* (our intuition enriching our experience), *the manifestation within mystery* (our experience enriching our intuition), *the naming of the un-*

*named* (the infusion of our reasoning consciousness with our intuitive consciousness), and *the un-naming of the named* (the dissolution of alienation from our reasoning consciousness).

What is implied here is nothing less than the healing of the split between the two hemispheres of our brain which have become separated, alienated and at war with each other during the past few thousand years. Practically speaking, this means, for example, the "artistification" of science, the "scientification" of art, the "ecumenicalization" of religion, and the spiritualization of life.

In the realm of *science*, this is a process which nuclear physics, more than any other scientific discipline, has initiated. In a more advanced evolutionary stage, it will mean the transformation of our fixed and objective hierarchical structures into objective-subjective interactive processes. For example, our present linearly and hierarchically structured languages are likely to transform into a music-language, capable of communicating subtle differentiations and simultaneities of experience, reasoning and feeling.

In the realm of *art*, the Great Integrity implies the "artistification" of life and the gradual disappearance of our old-age art "closets" such as museums and performance halls. In a more advanced evolutionary stage, we can imagine the transformation of musical and dance composition to improvisation, of painting framed pictures to the "artistification" of our entire environment.

In the realm of *religion*, we can look forward to the ecumenical dissolution of sects, dogmas and superstitions since they create a rigor mortis of the mind, emotions and spirit. In an even more advanced evolutionary stage we might achieve the spiritualization of every aspect of life and consciousness.

This verse welcomes the disappearance of all boundaries among art, science and religion as the walls and premises of every discipline dissolve into a higher consciousness and an uncompromising integrity of human relations and life experience. Therefore, *when these interpenetrations are in full attendance, we will pass the gates of naming notions in our journey toward transcendence.*

# *Verse* 2

## RELATIVITY

We know beauty because there is ugly.
We know good because there is evil.
Being and not being,
having and not having,
create each other.

Difficult and easy,
long and short,
high and low,
define each other,
just as before and after follow each other.

The dialectic of sound
gives voice to music,
always transforming "is" from "was"
as the ancestors of "to be".

The wise teach without telling,
allow without commanding,
have without possessing,
care without claiming.

In this way we harvest eternal importance
because we never announce it.

## VERSE 2 COMMENTARY

This verse celebrates the relativity of reality, thereby aligning itself with modern science, especially Einstein's theory of relativity. The corollary is a rejection of fundamentalism and absolutism. *Verse 2* is a poetic reminder that one of our twenty-first-century requisites is to transcend all superstitions. To believe that our world today is just as God created it and has never ever changed, nor will ever change, shuts the door to transformation. Such a premise locks us into the inequities of the past that were predicated on a condition of scarcity and a division between a minority who can fulfill their needs and a majority who cannot. Twenty-first-century technology makes *have* and *have-not* inequities, as well as their rationales, anachronistic.

Lao Tzu's theory of relativity suggests new paradigms of consciousness. He implies that when there will be no gluttony, there will be no starvation, when there will be no rich, there will be no poor. That is self-evident. However, what does it mean to say that when there will be no ugly, there will be no beauty, and that when there will be no evil, there will be no good?

It means that beauty and good will no longer be expressed as compensatory for the ugly and the evil in our life experience. It means that we will not any longer have to express *beauty* separated from life as art, nor *good* separated from life as a spiritual expression. It is possible that twenty-first-century life will rediscover the harmony between our environment and us, and the harmony among each other, and within us.

It is this harmony that will be *good* and *beautiful* only as seen from our current perspective. But from a future perspective, *good* and *beautiful* as alienated compensations will not exist because evil and ugly will not exist. What we today call *good* and *beautiful* will simply permeate the character of life.

If *beauty* will no longer be separable from life, then we

may expect that, eventually, there will no longer be concert halls and museums, since the music and art of life will be inherent in all the sounds, movements and patterns of ordinary life, and will be expressed by every one of us, not just a specialist who creates beauty for us such as the professional musician and artist. We can imagine that some day every mode of communication might be spontaneously musical and poetic, every movement might be a dance, every object we create – a visual delight, all expressing the integral and actualizing character of life.

Similarly, in the distant future, we may not have need for churches, temples and mosques since life itself may become spiritual in all its forms, activities and expressions.

In such a world of the future, the teacher and the student might be so in tune with each other that they will be able to *teach without telling*. Each of us may become so in tune with every other person that we may spontaneously *allow without commanding*. To the extent that our lives issue from material and spiritual abundance, will we be free to *have without possessing* and *care without claiming*, and because in this new condition, we can expect to give and receive love freely, our egos will no longer be starved. *In this way, we* (will) *harvest eternal importance because we* (will) *never* (need to) *announce it*.

# *Verse 3*

## TEMPERING

Overpraising the gifted
leads to contentiousness.
Overvaluing the precious
invites stealing.
Craving the desirable
loses contentment.

The natural person
desires without craving
and acts without excess.

By not doing,
everything is done.

## VERSE 3 COMMENTARY

不尚賢使民不爭不貴難得之貨使民不為
盜不見可欲使心不亂是以聖人之治也虛其心實
其腹弱其志強其骨常使民無知無欲使夫知
者不敢為也為無為則無不治矣

Excess is rooted in deprivation. When our talents are not appreciated we endlessly seek praising. When we are denied the essentials of life, we overvalue the precious. When our physical, emotional and spiritual needs are unfulfilled, we develop desperate cravings because we are starved.

Freedom from deprivation will allow us to function effortlessly. Only then will everything be done as natural expressions of our life needs and rhythms rather than as compensations for our deprivations.

# *Verse* 4

## THE GREAT INTEGRITY

The Great Integrity is an endless abyss,
Yet, it is the inexhaustibly fertile
source of the universe.

It blunts all sharpness,
unties the entangled,
and merges with the dust!

Hidden but ever present –
this parent of the gods –
whose child may it be?

## VERSE 4 COMMENTARY

As the creator of all mythologies and realities, the Great Integrity (Tao) is the paradox that transcends all states of being. It is the *endless abyss, yet it is the inexhaustibly fertile source of the universe*. The Great Integrity is the mediator of every state. *It blunts all sharpness* and *unties the entangled*. It not only creates, transcends and modifies, but the Great Integrity itself *merges with the dust*, that state to which all matter ultimately returns.

In Western theology nothing precedes God. But according to Lao Tzu, the Great Integrity is the *source of the universe*, including all ideas as well as the *10,000 phenomena*. The gods are thereby also children of the Great Integrity. Lao Tzu goes on to ask the ultimate epistemological question: where did the Great Integrity come from – *whose child may it be*?

His implied answer is that beyond the finite limitations of our perceptions is an infinity of time, space, energy and matter, which, by definition, has no beginning. Therefore nothing precedes the Great Integrity, and it is nobody's child.

Such a concept transcends contemporary religion and science both of which harness us to the quantified paradigms of the past few thousand years. The transcendence of these precepts is requisite to our entering the higher evolutionary phase that the twenty-first century promises as a potential for our species self-realization.

# *Verse* 5

## YIN AND YANG

Yin and yang aren't sentimental.
They exist without moralizing.
They act regardless of our wishes
within the ebb and flow
of every pregnant moment.

The space between yin and yang
is like a bellows –
empty, yet infinitely full.
The more it yields,
the more it fills.

Countless words
count less
than the silent balance
between yin and yang.

天地不仁以萬物為芻。狗聖人不仁以百姓為芻
狗天地之間其猶橐籥乎虛而不屈動而愈
出多言數窮不如守中

## VERSE 5 COMMENTARY

Yin and yang, like heaven and earth, is a metaphor for all that exists. We are reminded here that existence is not sentimental. The course of events does not simply follow our wishes or prayers.

Moreover, the harder we try to force events to conform to our moralizations, the less likely our success. On the other hand, the more we yield to the rhythms (*bellows*) of life, the greater our fruition. How often Lao Tzu bids us to put aside our ideological predilections so that we may be free to ebb and flow with the new opportunities *of every pregnant moment*.

Thus – *Countless words* (our exhortations) *count less than the silent* (existential) *balance between yin and yang*.

# Verse 6

## LIFE'S SPIRIT

The spirit of life
never dies.

It is the infinite gateway
to mysteries within mysteries.

It is the seed of yin,
the spark of yang.

Always elusive,
endlessly available.

谷神不死是謂玄牝玄牝之門是謂天地根
緜緜若存用之不勤

## VERSE 6 COMMENTARY

The spirit of life is infinite, mysterious, inexhaustible and both passive (yin) and active (yang). It is the non-dualistic aspect of spirit that separates the Great Integrity from all religious precepts of spirit. There is a corollary separation of the Great Integrity from modern science, which also harbors dualistic premises.

However, twenty-first century meta-scientific spirituality is already seeded in molecular physics and in an ecumenical consciousness. Our twenty-first-century opportunities are strewn with the materialization of the spiritual and the spiritualization of the material as we de-dichotomize all the cobwebs of our dualistic mythologies, allowing us to experience life as spontaneity and free of ideological filters.

# *Verse* 7

## MODESTY

The Great Integrity, having had no birth,
expresses its immortality
without pronouncements.

The wise are heard
through their silence,
always self-full through selflessness.

### VERSE 7 COMMENTARY

When we no longer have to respond to the compulsive alternating bulimic demands and anorexic deprivations of our battered egos, then we will fulfill ourselves naturally and silently. Just as the Great Integrity expresses its immortality without pronouncements, we will then become capable of self-fulness through selflessness.

## *Verse* 8

# THE HIGHEST GOOD

The highest good is like water,
nourishing life effortlessly,
flowing without prejudice
to the lowliest places.

It springs from all
who nourish their community
with a benevolent heart
as deep as an abyss,
who are incapable of lies and injustices,
who are rooted in the earth,
and whose natural rhythms of action
play midwife to the highest good
of each joyful moment.

## VERSE 8 COMMENTARY

From an evolutionary point of view, we can differentiate four stages of goodness:

(1) The goodness that was expressed in the communality of tribal times, during which survival depended upon the total cooperation among all members of the tribe.

(2) The goodness that Confucianism and other religions advocate as an expression of the more altruistic side of our personalities. The assumption in these advocacies is that goodness requires an effort, a struggle against our supposedly innate tendencies to be selfish and sinful.

(3) The goodness that is expressed in this verse which implies that while both goodness and badness coexist, that it is goodness that flows effortlessly like water, because it is goodness that is more at the core of nature.

(4) The goodness that transcends goodness when, in our future evolution, the polarization of good and bad might no longer exist. (See *Verse 2*.) Instead, we can envisage the actualization of a socially enhanced inherent humanity. It is only this fourth type of goodness that fully expresses the Great Integrity.

# *Verse 9*

## OVERFULFILLMENT

Keep filling your bowl,
and it will spill over.

Keep sharpening your knife,
and it will blunt.

Keep hoarding gold in your house,
and you will be robbed.

Keep seeking approval,
and you will be chained.

The Great Integrity leads to actualization,
never overfulfillment.

## VERSE 9 COMMENTARY

Our culture conditions us to keep filling our bowl even after it is full, to keep accumulating more money even after we have enough to meet all our needs, to keep reaching out for more accolades even after we have been fully acknowledged.

No other species ever seeks more than it needs. To do so is a pathological symptom that negates the very fulfillments we crave. If we reject Freud's thesis that human beings are biologically self-destructive, what is the explanation for these self-negating behaviors?

When our bowl is the community bowl that we fill and use collectively, we never overfill it.

When our knife is the community knife that we sharpen and use together, we never oversharpen it.

When our possessions are community possessions that we gather and use for each other's mutual benefit, we never miserly hoard them.

When love is freely expressed, naturally nurturing each member of the community, we never seek it with insatiable desperation.

But in our culture, each of our bowls is our own bowl, competing with every other for filling. Each of our possessions is our own possession, acquired competitively in the heartless marketplace. Because we have sacrificed cooperation for competition, the *cash-nexus* has taken the place of sharing mutual concern and love, generating instead – inequities, hostilities and inhumanities among us.

However, ours is that unique evolutionary moment when we can liberate ourselves from all the inequities of the past. One aspect of this liberation is the acquiring of a new Great Integrity consciousness that rejects the excesses of the past several thousand years. We can now transform our way of life so that we are no longer addicted to over-filling our bowls, over-sharpening our knives, over-accumulating possessions, and over-extending our demands for attention and love. Celebrate the Great Integrity as the pathway to actualization in which our self and social components will be mutually supportive and no longer in conflict with each other!

# *Verse* 10

## LIMITATIONS

When embracing the unity
of mind, body, emotions
and spiritual being,
can we transcend our fragmentations
without leaving a trace?

When Qi Gong sculpts sinew suppleness,
can our flesh become soft
as a new-born babe?

Can we cleanse the inner vision,
leaving mind in spiritual purity?

Can our affairs of the heart,
and our affairs of state
be so unconditional
that we grant unqualified permissibility?

Can the gate to yin be opened
without inviting yang?

Can our reasoning mind
be purged of coercion,
allowing our heart its unfettered joy?

Can we act like every other species,
seeking no reward,
taking no pride,
guiding without enslaving?

Such is our vision of the Great Integrity
on whose path we have at last
planted both feet,
ready to move, step by step,
until we arrive at the great unfettered gate.

## VERSE 10 COMMENTARY

There are two principal implications about our limitations in this hymn to the Great Integrity:

(1) The universal limitations of reality are relative rather than absolute. The answer to every question posed in this verse is therefore, *no* because nothing exists in its pure ideal form, and because there can be no yin without its opposite, yang.

(2) However, the conditions that define our time as the age of transition, lead us to answer these questions with a qualified, *yes*. We can now *begin* this journey, but our generations will never be able to fully actualize the Great Integrity.

# *Verse* 11

## THE IMPORTANCE OF WHAT IS NOT

We join thirty spokes
to the hub of a wheel,
yet it's the center hole
that drives the chariot.

We shape clay
to birth a vessel,
yet it's the hollow within
that makes it useful.

We chisel doors and windows
to construct a room,
yet it's the inner space
that makes it livable.

Thus do we create what is
to use what is not.

## VERSE 11 COMMENTARY

It may seem that Lao Tzu in this verse advocates *what is not* over *what is*. Similarly, he seems to advocate *not doing* over *doing*. It would appear that he announces *nothingness* as the goal of life. To make a pun, *nothing* could be further from his intent. In fact, he celebrates the maximal doing with the minimal effort.

Lao Tzu's *nothingness* is not a reference to the absence of content, but rather to the absence of aggression. He does not worship inaction, sleep, death or the withdrawal from a responsible life. In this verse, although he focuses on the inactive part as being most functional, clearly there would be no inactive part without having created the other parts. There is no center hole without making the spokes and hub, no hollow in the vessel without making the vessel, no inner space without constructing the walls, doors and windows that define it.

Lao Tzu rather reminds us that there is always a yin (the passive and empty component) that coexists with the yang (the active and shaping component). The two together provide the means to total action, total responsibility, *lifefulness*, and *lovefulness*. He focuses on the yin component in this verse as a metaphor for establishing the greater relative importance of nurturing (yin) compared with acting (yang), which is often expressed as aggression.

More specifically, the main reason we tend to forget or denigrate the yin part of all processes is that the yang part in our lives has become dominant and excessive, tending to express itself as coercion. This condition has defined our lives since ancient times. Only the forms of coercion have changed. But to divorce aggression from action does not leave emptiness, but the space for natural action, that action whose mother is our humanity and whose father is necessity, and which therefore is born in full innocence.

*The importance of what is not* defines the classical paradigm called *enlightenment*. Specifically, meditation requires thoughtlessness. However, Lao Tzu does not advocate emptying the mind as an ultimate goal, but rather as a means of cleansing it of its garbage and of preparing it for a more holistic, more human and less alienated content.

# Verse 12

## CHOICES

Colors can make us blind!
Music can make us deaf!
Flavors can destroy our taste!
Possessions can close our options!
Racing can drive us mad
and its rewards obstruct our peace!

Thus, the wise
fill the inner gut
rather than the eyes,
always sacrificing the superficial
for the essential.

## VERSE 12 COMMENTARY

五色令人目盲五音令人耳聾五味令人口爽
馳騁田獵令人心發狂難得之貨令人行妨是
以聖人為腹不為目故去彼取此

There is no intention here to sing the praises of asceticism. That idea is more in tune with Confucianism and Christianity.

Lao Tzu is mainly calling our attention to the relative importance of the inner compared with the outer, the essential compared with the superficial.

Furthermore, in excess, sights, sounds and flavors can destroy our senses. Certainly, our high-profile crass billboards, our violent TV and films, our high-decibel junk music and denatured chemicalized "foods" qualify to make us blind and deaf, and to destroy our taste.

The last stanza spells it out without ambiguity by favoring the "inner gut", a metaphor for our *essentiality*, over the "eyes", a metaphor for our outer *superficiality*.

# *Verse* 13

## IDENTITY

Accolades can usher in
great trouble for your body.
Censure can herald misery.

Why can favor and disfavor
both be harmful?

Because both accolades and censure,
when filtered through self as ego,
always place us in jeopardy.

But when the universe becomes your self,
when you love th[illegible]
all reality become[illegible]
reinventing you a[illegible]

Only then, will you transcend tense
to fully be here now.
Only then, no harm
will the universe proffer
nor you to her,
for you will be
not you but she
and both – the universal Great Integrity.

## VERSE 13 COMMENTARY

Both praise and criticism can result in harm when we relate to the world through an insatiable ego. That is because when so doing, each honor generates a need for an even greater honor, and each dishonor generates a lower self-esteem.

However, when we identify ourselves as inextricable parts of the universe, rather than as our separate individual egos, accolades and criticisms, successes and failures, no longer have power over us. The transformation from predominant ego-identity to predominant community-identity is one of our joyful pathways to the Great Integrity.

# Verse 14

## BEYOND REASON

That which we look at
but cannot see is the invisible.

That which we listen to
but cannot hear is the inaudible.

That which we reach for
but cannot grasp is the intangible.

Beyond reason,
these three merge,
contradicting experience.

Their rising side isn't bright.
Their setting side isn't dark.

Sense-less, unnamable,
they return to the realms of nothingness.

Form without form,
image without image,
indefinable, ineluctable, elusive.

Confronting them, you see no beginning.
Following them, you see no end.

Yet, riding the plowless plow
can seed the timeless Tao,
harvesting the secret
transcendence of the Now.

## VERSE 14 COMMENTARY

What is beyond sight, hearing and touching – even beyond reason and experience? A world without the rising light or the setting darkness, where there is neither form nor image, neither beginning nor end.

It is the elusive indefinable and paradoxical Great Integrity of the universe, the Tao, which transcends time, space and matter.

What use for the Great Integrity do we human beings have when we are absorbed in acquiring *ten thousand* possessions? None. Even worse, it subverts our false values, premises, goals and institutions. The Great Integrity is an invitation to the most radical transformation of our lives and consciousness. It is a challenge to transcend civilization as fragmentation and acquisitiveness, an open door to re-enter life with an uncompromised humanity, totally synergistic with the universe.

Because it is subversive, the Great Integrity appears in disguise, as a secret transcendence.

# *Verse* 15

## LINKING WITH ANCIENT TIMES

In ancient times
the people knew the Great Integrity
with subtlety and profundity.

Because they are so unfathomable to us,
we can describe the ancients
only with great effort.

They were –
cautious as those crossing an icy stream,
wary as those surrounded by dangers,
dignified as guests,
yielding as melting ice,
innocent as virgin wood,
open and broad as valleys,
merging freely as muddy water.

But today, who can remain patient
while the mud so gradually clears?
Who can remain still
while the moment for action
so slowly emerges?

Who?
We observers of the Great Integrity,
who in our times,
like those ancients,
when never seeking fulfillment,
are never unfulfilled.

## VERSE 15 COMMENTARY

Ancient times for us twenty-first-century readers of the *Tao Te Ching* represents a *double entendre*. We can stand back with Lao Tzu, living in the sixth century BCE and view his ancient times, by which he means tribal times and perhaps also the first one thousand years of Chinese civilization, that is, the era of the three first legendary emperors. We can also stand back from our own twenty-first century. Then, ancient times for us is Lao Tzu's own time. He says that the ancients lived so long ago that they are unfathomable and can be described only with great effort. Since today we are much further removed from tribal times, both chronologically and culturally, we might find the seven metaphors of the third stanza even more unfathomable. Like Lao Tzu, when I speak to my contemporaries of the Great Integrity, they laugh. They say people have never been like that. They have always been selfish and competitive. What they mean, of course, is that this is the way people have been during the past few thousand years of recorded history.

The fourth stanza returns us to a time contemporary with the writing of the *Tao Te Ching* and expresses the impatience that the people then had in acquiring a Tao consciousness. Now, you might say that we deserve to be more impatient. Although the intuitive Great Integrity of tribal times is more distanced for us than for Lao Tzu, today we are within grasp of being able to consciously create a planetary Great Integrity. Yet, paradoxically and frustratingly, the patterns of the past cling ever more desperately, the closer we come to replacing them.

# *Verse* 16

## TRANQUILLITY

Allow the heart to empty itself
of all turmoil!
Retrieve the utter tranquillity of mind
from which you issued.

Although all forms are dynamic,
and we all grow and transform,
each of us is compelled
to return to our root.
Our root is quietude.

To fully return to our root
is to be enlightened.
Never to experience tranquillity
is to act blindly,
a sure path to disaster.

To know tranquillity is to embrace all.
To embrace all is to be just.
Justice is the foundation for wholeness.
Wholeness is the Great Integrity.
The Great Integrity
is the infinite fulfilling itself.

## VERSE 16 COMMENTARY

Ever since we human beings acquired the capacity to feel separate from all that is *Not-I*, a process sociologists call *alienation*, we have lost the tranquillity that is inherent in living as an inextricable part of nature. This process escalated during the evolution of what we euphemistically call *civilization*, the predominant form of society during these past few millennia. In civilizations, we not only became *separated* from all that is *Not-I*, but we became the *enemies* of each other, of our environment, and even of ourselves. Consequently, we have had to invent cultural compensations for our loss of wholeness and for our destructive social relations. Religion (holiness) and the arts (creativity) were developed as virtual institutions that help us to momentarily re-experience the harmony and tranquillity that is no longer inherent in everyday life.

Here Lao Tzu reminds us that it is the nature of nature to emerge from and return to the peace of undifferentiated oneness, that is, to the Great Integrity, and the failure to do so is fatal.

# *Verse* 17

## LEADERS

There are four types of leaders:
The best leader
is indistinguishable from the will
of those who selected her.
The next best leader
enjoys the love and praise of the people.
The poor leader
rules through coercion and fear.
And the worst leader
is a tyrant despised by the multitudes
who are the victims of his power.

What a world of difference
among these leaders!
In the last two types,
what is done is without sincerity or trust –
only coercion.

In the second type,
there is a harmony
between the leader and the people.
In the first type,
whatever is done happens so naturally
that no one presumes to take the credit!

## VERSE 17 COMMENTARY

We are familiar with all these kinds of leaders except for the first type. In the early days of their revolutions, Thomas Jefferson, Vladimir Lenin, Mao Tse-Tung and Fidel Castro were the second type. Josef Stalin ruled through coercion and fear. And Hitler was certainly a tyrant who was despised by hundreds of millions of people throughout the world.

Those leaders who rule by fear, coercion and tyranny do not acquire and sustain their power simply by some mysterious force. Such leaders require an army of people who are willing to serve as enforcers of injustice. Furthermore, and what may at first consideration be astonishing, such leaders first come to power through at least the tacit approval of the majority, even though it leads to their victimization. How can such irrationality envelop an entire nation like a plague? Some answers are suggested by Lao Tzu in the next three verses (18, 19 and 20), which elucidate some of the consequences of losing the Great Integrity.

Where do we find examples of the first type of leaders – the kind whose leadership is so indistinguishable from the will of those who select them that no one presumes to take the credit for anything that is done? Indeed, such leaders are not to be found anywhere in the written history of civilizations. Only pre-civilization leaders in democratic and egalitarian tribal societies had no need, nor possibility to take credit for the interactive cooperative efforts and accomplishments of the entire community.

In Lao Tzu's time there was no way that such a totally democratic community could re-emerge. That is possible only today now that we have a technology that can provide the material and cultural needs of all people on our planet. For us to continue to make war with each other, and to continue to elect leaders who carry out inhuman sectarian acts, is now a social insanity.

# *Verse 18*

## THE PARADOXES OF ABANDONING THE GREAT INTEGRITY

When the Great Integrity was abandoned,
humanity and justice appeared.

When knowledge and teachers appeared,
hypocrisy was
their inevitable accompaniment.

When relationships lost their harmony,
filial piety and parental affection
were suddenly birthed.

When a nation succumbs
to chaos and corruption,
patriotic politicians are always at hand
announcing themselves.

## VERSE 18 COMMENTARY

When civilization exchanged the Great Integrity for the universal fragmentation of all entities, integrity was sacrificed at the altar of measuring and pricing each fragment.

This process of integrity dismemberment is rationalized by logical ideologies, which are intellectualizations that are severed from holistic life experience. Accordingly, Lao Tzu ignores these vested static logical illusions, preferring to speak in the paradoxical language of processes and transformations.

In this verse, it is implied that many people celebrate "humanity" and "justice" as ideal universal virtues. But Lao Tzu knows that when the Great Integrity was abandoned, *inhumanity* and *injustice* became universal experiences. He also reminds us that we have come to know humanity only as a release from the inhumanity that dominates life.

In fact, there can be no awareness of humanity without inhumanity, no justice without injustice, right without wrong. As *Verse 2 – Relativity* points out, we know beauty because there is ugly and good because there is evil. The Great Integrity does not know justice because it does not know injustice.

This verse thereby implies part of the answer to the question in the previous *Verse 17 – Leaders*: Why should a majority contribute to their own victimization? One way is by succumbing to the ideologies that rationalize inequities and injustices as though they are inherent in life itself rather than the consequences of selling our holistic souls (the Great Integrity) to the fragmentized marketplace. By accepting these ideologies as universal truths, we accommodate to our own shackles.

# *Verse* 19

## THE PARADOXES OF RETURNING TO THE GREAT INTEGRITY

Banish the intellectual!
Discard knowledge!
We will all benefit a hundredfold!

Eliminate all institutions
of charity and justice!
We can then return
to our natural love for each other.

Let everyone be released
from our addictions
to shrewdness and profit!
Then, thievery will disappear!

These three negate the Great Integrity.
But to negate these negations
is insufficient.
Three affirmations are also necessary.

The first is to embrace
simplicity and integrity.
The second is to consume
only the needs of our body and soul.
The third is to allow our love and concern
for others to define our essentiality.

## VERSE 19 COMMENTARY

Lao Tzu suggests that we discard knowledge and eliminate charity and justice. He doesn't ask us to discard ignorance and eliminate selfishness and injustice as we might expect from someone who is dedicated to improving life. There are two implications in Lao Tzu's carefully selected terminology:

(1) For Lao Tzu, it is not enough only to *reduce* ignorance, selfishness and injustice. These despicable characteristics need to be entirely eliminated. When ignorance no longer exists, there cannot be intellectuals who are the only knowledgeable ones. When no one is deprived, charity will have no use and will disappear from our lives and vocabularies. When injustice disappears, the concept of justice will have no meaning.

(2) In a world in which ideologies function as rationales for inequities, logic can be utilized manipulatively. Lao Tzu's frequent use of paradox (*Discard knowledge and we will all benefit a hundredfold*!) is a way of shocking us and shaking up our old modes of thinking so that we become open to an alternative consciousness. For us, it is also an in-your-face rejection of Platonian and Cartesian logic as rigid, mechanistic and anachronistic.

This verse not only points out the obstacles to our experiencing life holistically, it also declares three prerequisites: 1) to embrace simplicity and integrity, 2) to consume only the needs of our body and soul, and 3) to allow our love and concern for others (and, of course, for ourselves) to define our identities.

# Verse 20

## THE SADNESS OF SUPERFICIALITIES AND OF THE UNFULFILLED GREAT INTEGRITY

It is sometimes deeply depressing
to be a rebel,
knowing that we can never share
most people's way of life,
nor can they share ours.

Schooling stuffs the brains
of our children with trivia.
The more the trivia,
the more their anxieties.
They indoctrinate the children
to believe that the consequences are grave
when they fail to distinguish
"good" from "evil",

and agreement from disagreement.
What gross nonsense!

To escape the rubbish
of all this so-called knowledge,
in the winter, people run
to the great feasts of lamb, pork and ox,
and they climb high in the mountains
to view the first signs of spring.

We are so different!
Having no desire for the trivialities,
nor for their compensations,
we are like infants
not yet knowing how to laugh!
Ever wandering, and having no home
to which we may return.

While most people are obsessed
with superficialities,
we feel empty.
While most people feel

they know so much,
we feel simple-minded.
While most people believe
they live happily
in the best of all possible worlds,
we are despaired to witness this world!

It is so painful to know
that we will always be outsiders,
endlessly moving like the ocean,
aimlessly blowing like the wind.

While we fear what others fear,
we don't treasure what others treasure.
Our treasure is the Great Integrity.
However, until it is shared,
it will not be the Universal Integrity,
for we are part of them,
and they are part of us.

## VERSE 20 COMMENTARY

How often we who are rebels have despaired! We identify with Lao Tzu and his frustrations. We have so often shared his sadness and his discouragement of not being accepted by either the power elite or by the majority who are often cleverly manipulated to identify with the very views that victimize them.

Of course, those who have the power and the privileges of wealth are opposed to any radical changes. They want to conserve their power and privileges, so they are known as conservatives, though some pretend to side with the people, giving themselves liberal sounding names.

The privileged elite also controls the main belief systems that rationalize the inequities of power. Today, they do so by owning and controlling the main media that mold the views of the public. Even more fundamentally, they control the jobs that provide the money that buys all the necessities of life. No wonder we have a hard time being heard! No wonder we feel isolated and alienated from the main streams of social, political and economic life!

Such have been the frustrations of us rebels since the time of Lao Tzu. But, at last, today we have an alternative. We can form a global community and return to the Great

Integrity when children will no longer be indoctrinated with trivia, and adults will no longer suffer the inhumanities that are masked by overindulgent escapes. It makes us wish that Lao Tzu were among us to appreciate and celebrate these new opportunities. But, of course, he is – in these very verses!

# *Verse* 21

## THE GREAT INTEGRITY IS A PARADOX

The Great Integrity is a paradox.
It is inherent in the universe,
yet its form is so illusive.
It is the Vital Essence of every entity,
yet nothing announces
its essential character.

The Great Integrity was apparent
before time, space and matter
appeared to separate.
How can we re-mind
and re-infuse ourselves
with this very touchstone
of all essentialities and connections?

By re-fusing time, space and matter
with the spiritualization
of our materiality,
and with the materialization
of our spirituality.

Then, when our dualities and numeralities
become blurred and forgotten,
the Great Integrity will re-emerge in forms
of such incredible depths and dimensions
of enlightenment
precisely because our temporary
fragmentary consciousness
created a multi-millennial amnesia.

## VERSE 21 COMMENTARY

In this case, I took some liberties with the translation to bring Lao Tzu's essential idea of the Great Integrity as paradox into contemporary terms and issues. While Lao Tzu refers to substance, essence, and belief and the fragmentation of all things and ideas, I translate this as the separation of time, space and matter. Of course, the integrity of energy, time, space and matter which Lao Tzu intuits and calls the Great Integrity has been scientifically verified by Einstein, with its specific relations defined by his well-known $e=mc^2$ equation.

Even by Lao Tzu's time, dualism and quantifications began to replace the Great Integrity in the categorizing and enumerating of the "ten thousand things". Of course, modern institutions and science since the time of Descartes and Newton greatly escalated the process. Gradually, competition and fragmentation began more and more to appear as the nature of nature and of the universe, thereby rationalizing the organization of societies into competing units as natural and inevitable. The accompanying philosophies dichotomized mind and matter, spirituality and materiality, and provided the ideological basis for the separation of religion from science. Each philosophy and religion developed its own explanation for how misery and inhumanity are inherent in the nature of everything that doesn't reside in heaven.

But it was this very fragmentized consciousness that produced modern science and technology, which, in turn, now provides the material basis for the possibility for planetary abundance. As we approach the establishment of a possible egalitarian planetary community, the dualistic underpinnings of life as relative scarcity can begin to crumble, allowing us to spiritualize our materiality and materialize our spirituality.

We are poised to set foot on the social and personal paths toward re-achieving the Great Integrity which Lao Tzu's contemporaries could realize only in their meditations and dreams. Here's to the multi-millennial period of Great Integrity amnesia, which paradoxically was our historical prerequisite to re-achieving the Great Integrity itself on a higher level than nature first expressed it. Before human beings, the Great Integrity was the unconscious common experience of all life. Now we human beings can re-create it and live it consciously, a unique capability of our species.

# *Verse* 22

## CELEBRATE PARADOX!

No-thing remains itself.
Each prepares the path to its opposite.

To be ready for wholeness,
first be fragmented.
To be ready for rightness,
first be wronged.
To be ready for fullness, first be empty.
To be ready for renewal, first be worn out.
To be ready for success, first fail.
To be ready for doubt, first be certain.

Because the wise observe the world
through the Great Integrity,
they know they are not knowledgeable.
Because they do not perceive
only through their perceptions,

they do not judge
this right and that wrong.
Because they do not delight in boasting,
they are appreciated.
Because they do not announce
their superiority,
they are acclaimed.
Because they never compete,
no one can compete with them.

Verily, fragmentation
prepares the path to wholeness,
the mother of all origins and realizations.

曲則全枉則直窪則盈弊則新少則得多
則惑是以聖人抱一為天下式不自見故明不
自是故彰不自伐故有功不自矜故長夫惟
不爭故天下莫能與之爭古之所謂曲則全
者豈虛言哉故誠全而歸之

## VERSE 22 COMMENTARY

This verse is an elaboration on paradox of the previous four verses. It seems that now we might be able to recover the Great Integrity precisely and paradoxically because we have suffered for so many centuries as victims of its loss.

Paradox and the transformation of any entity into its opposite is not only the nature of the Great Integrity, but of its own rebirth, and indeed, of all natural processes.

# *Verse* 23

## SINCERITY

Speak few words, but say them
with quietude and sincerity,
and they will be long lasting,
for a raging wind cannot blow all morning,
nor a sudden rainstorm
last throughout the day.

Why is this so?
Because it is the nature of the sky
and the earth to be frugal.
Even human beings
cannot alter this nature
without suffering the consequences.

When we sincerely follow the ethical path,
we become one with it.

When we become one
with the ethical path,
it embraces us.

When we completely lose our way,
we become one with loss.
When we become one with loss,
loss embraces us.

When we sincerely follow
the Great Integrity,
we become one with it.
When we are one with the
Great Integrity,
it embraces us.

But when nothing is done sincerely,
no-thing and no one embraces us.

## VERSE 23 COMMENTARY

The actions of a sincere person speak for themselves. But when there is a contradiction between words and deeds, the space between them needs to be filled with mountains of rationalizations. Therefore, those who are sincere speak few words. Those who speak loquaciously are not sincere.

Very simply put, the Great Integrity and insincerity are as incompatible as honesty and dishonesty. When we choose insincerity and dishonesty there is always a price that we pay: to be left lonely and "unembraced" in our exile from the Great Integrity.

# *Verse* 24

## AVOIDING VOIDS

Standing on tiptoe
will only make you tipsy,
Walking with long strides
will not allow a long walk.
Shining the light on yourself
will never enlighten you.
Being self-righteous
precludes you from being right.
Boasting about yourself
will never boost your eminence.
Parading yourself
parodies leadership.

Tao consciousness
avoids the cultivation
of all these ego bloated voids.

# VERSE 24 COMMENTARY

跂者不立跨者不行自見者不明自是者不彰自伐者無功自矜者不長其於道也曰餘食贅行物或惡之故有道者不處也

All our artificialities, superficialities, and needs for parading our egos are compensations for the Great Void that derives from living loveless lives.

When this void will be transcended, our individual rhythms and goals will become coincident with our ecologies. This is what Lao Tzu means by the return of the Great Integrity when self and social actualizations will fill all the ego-bloated voids, releasing us from the compensatory addictions that we now so desperately cultivate.

# *Verse* 25

## NAMING THE NAMELESS

What preceded life?
The earth.
What preceded the earth?
The universe.
What preceded the universe?
The soundless and shapeless
origin of origins,
ever transforming
and having no beginning nor end.

This Mother of the universe
is boundless, and nameless.
But if we wanted to share with you
anything about this remarkable
non-executing executor,
we must invent a name for it.

We will call it the *Tao*
because Tao means *great*.
Incredibly great
because it occupies infinite space,
being fully present in the whole universe,
and in every infinitesimal particle.

Because this Great Integrity
created the universe,
and the universe created the earth,
and the earth created us,
we are all incredibly great.

Life derives
from the nature of the earth.
The earth derives
from the nature of the universe.
The universe derives
from the nature of the Great Integrity.
And the Great Integrity
is the omnipresent, omnigenous omniform,

the universal material
and spiritual substance,
the holoversal interlinkage
and coition of existence.

## VERSE 25 COMMENTARY

Here in this remarkable verse, we find Lao Tzu occupying (though never smugly) a more advanced scientific position than the most advanced science of the twenty-first century!

Certainly, physics, in both relativity and quantum theory, represents the most comprehensive analysis of the nature of the universe we live in compared with any of the other sciences. However, in macrophysics (relativity theory), even Einstein's $e=mc^2$, which demonstrated the inextricable relation of energy, matter and the speed of light, has not allowed physicists to go the full way with Lao Tzu who concluded 2,700 years ago that there was never a beginning of time, matter, or space, and that the Great Integrity is infinite. Physicists, still search for the "beginning" of the universe, and now posit the "Big Bang" theory in their seemingly obstinate clinging to the last vestige of the particularistic Newtonian-Cartesian paradigm.

In twenty-first century microphysics (quantum theory), the search for the Holy Grail – the smallest particle of matter – has also still not been abandoned. Once thought to be the mighty atom, quantum physics has further reduced the fundamental fragment of the universe first to electrons, positrons and neutrons, then to neutrinos and antineutrinos, then further to photons, hadrons, quarks, antiquarks and mesons. Finally, quantum physics has posited that the particles themselves are not the most irreducible fragment of matter, but that even smaller components can be discerned as waves, specifically, as *superstrings*.

What indeed may very well become the most advanced scientific understanding of the nature of the universe is Lao Tzu's proposal of the Great Integrity where both the macro and the micro aspects meet in an irreducible infinitude without beginnings, endings or entities of any kind that are not related and interlinked.

# *Verse* 26

## SEDUCTIONS

Inner strength is the master
of all frivolities.
Tranquillity is the master
of all agitated emotions.

Those who succumb to frivolities
have lost their inner strength.
Those who succumb to agitated emotions
have lost their tranquillity.

The wise cultivate
inner strength and tranquillity.
That is why they are not seduced
by addictive temptations.

## VERSE 26 COMMENTARY

Living in a world before we have achieved the Great Integrity often challenges our inner strength and tranquillity, tempting us to give up these anchors to our human essence for addictive escapes from the stresses we are so frequently forced to confront.

We are reminded here that if we can embrace our inner strength and tranquillity when they are threatened by out-of-control addictions and emotions, we will stay the course toward the Great Integrity, and be grateful for having done so.

However, Lao Tzu invites no judgmental guilt or blame against those who don't hold fast, and for whatever reasons, let their addictions and run-away emotions hold sway at any moment. What on the surface here appears like a tautology is rather a profound insight that feelings of guilt or blame for losing one's way to the Great Integrity are themselves emotional toxins that can only more deeply enmesh us in our victimizations.

## *Verse* 27

# WISDOM IS EFFORTLESS MUTUALITY

The expert traveler
leaves no footprints.
The expert speaker
makes no mispronunciations.
The expert in calculation
needs no calculator.

The expert in closing things
needs no lock,
yet not one can open
what has been closed.
The expert in binding
uses no knots,
yet no one can pull apart
what has been bound.

The expert in caring for things
never wastes anything.
The expert at helping people
never abandons anyone.

These are the paths to enlightenment.
Those who arrive at their destination
teach those who are still on the path,
while those still on the path
are sources of wisdom for the teachers.

## VERSE 27 COMMENTARY

We are reminded here that sharing wisdom requires two basic qualities: 1) an enlightened expertise and 2) an effortless mutuality.

No matter how good a traveler you may be, if you do it under stress, you will indeed leave evidence of your dis-easeness. No matter how good a speaker you are, if there is a lack of agreement between you and your audience, you are likely to become inarticulate. No matter how good you are at counting, if you are counting something in which the others involved have an opposite vested interest, you are likely to make mistakes.

The wise who achieve an enlightened expertise in effortless mutuality teach those who are still on the path, but are always enriching themselves by learning from their students.

# *Verse* 28

## THE FUSION OF OPPOSITES

To know the masculine
and be true to the feminine
is to be the waterway of the world.

To be the waterway of the world
is to flow with the Great Integrity,
always swirling back
to the innocence of childhood.

To know yang
and to be true to yin
is to echo the universe.

To echo the universe
is to merge with the Great Integrity,
ever returning to the infinite.

To know praise
and be true to the lowly
is to be a model for the planet.

To be a model for the planet
is to express the Great Integrity
as the Primal Simplicity –
like an uncarved block.

When the uncarved block
goes to the craftsman,
it is transformed into something useful.

The wise craftsman
cuts as little as necessary
because he follows the Great Integrity.

## VERSE 28 COMMENTARY

*First*, we are reminded that all "ten-thousand things" of the universe are composed of opposites: masculine and feminine, yang and yin, high and low.

*Second*, Lao Tzu tells us that we should allow yin to be the dominant of the two opposites; that is, to know the masculine, but be true to the feminine, to know yang but be true to yin, to know praise but be true to the lowly.

*Third*, Lao Tzu observes that to merge with the Great Integrity is to ever return to the Primal Simplicity, and to make useful things by minimal interference with nature.

Yin predominated during the Neolithic era of communal matriarchal tribes. Our own age turned all this upside down. Throughout recorded history, our civilizations have been male dominated, competitive, nature-destructive, and ruled by those who were the most aggressive and war-like. How much more critical it is for us today to understand and to follow Lao Tzu's advice! Not to follow it in his time led to great unhappiness. Not to follow it in our time could lead to the end of our species on this planet.

# *Verse* 29

## WE ARE THE WORLD

Those who have most power and wealth
treat the planet as a thing to be possessed,
to be used and abused
according to their own dictates.
But the planet is a living organism,
a Great Spiritual Integrity.

To violate this Integrity
is certain to cull forth disaster
since each and every one of us
is an inherent part of this very organism.

All attempts to control the world
can only lead to its decimation
and to our own demise
since we are an inseparable part
of what we are senselessly trying to coerce.

Any attempt to possess the world
can only lead to its loss
and to our own dissolution
since we are an intrinsic part
of what we are foolishly trying to possess.

The world's pulse is our pulse.
The world's rhythms are our rhythms.
To treat our planet
with care, moderation and love
is to be in synchrony with ourselves
and to live in the Great Integrity.

## VERSE 29 COMMENTARY

No other species on our planet has the capability of creating the three illusions that we civilized human beings cultivate.

The *first* illusion is that we are separate from the world in which we live.

The *second* is that this world we live in is there for us to use and abuse according to our arbitrary wishes. We are the only arrogant species.

This arrogance was born out of a *third* illusion – that each of us is naturally in competition with other members of our own species. This illusion allows us to accept the institutionalization of the principle that most of us are here on this planet to serve those who establish hegemony over us.

Lao Tzu questions these three premises, and postulates that they are corruptions and violations of the nature of nature which is rooted in the very opposite paradigm that he calls the Great Integrity. In Lao Tzu's Great Integrity we are all inherently inseparable from our environment and from each other.

# *Verse* 30

## DEFENSE AND AGGRESSION

Those on the path of the Great Integrity
never use military force to conquer others.
Every aggressive act
harvests its own counter-terrorism.

Wherever the military marches,
the killing fields lay waste to the land,
yielding years of famine and misery.

When attacked, those on the path
of the Great Integrity
defend themselves benevolently,
never revenging.

Achieve success without arrogance,
without seeking glory,
and without violating others.

Aggression leaches
our strength and humanity,
subverting the Great Integrity,
and inviting disaster.

## VERSE 30 COMMENTARY

Again and again Lao Tzu denounces military aggression. However, he is not a pacifist. While justifying defense against aggression, he warns against acquiring the character of the aggressor. He cautions to engage in defense benevolently, never revenging nor violating others, never seeking glory nor acting arrogantly. Lastly, he reminds us that aggression leaches our strength and humanity, subverting the Great Integrity, and ultimately inviting disaster.

Of course, we twenty-first century-ites, being "blessed" with the ultimate nuclear, biological and chemical weapons, invite the ultimate disasters. Can we instead, embrace Lao Tzu's Great Integrity, and never again use military force to conquer others? For all of us, the answer to this question translates into the ultimate social choice: to be or not to be.

# Verse 31

## WAR

The finest weapons are the worst evils.
They are universally loathed.
Therefore, help guide your nation
to the non-aggressive path.

The wise hold steady
on the passive yin path.
Those who are aggressive
prefer the active yang.

Weapons are instruments of coercion
and devils of death.
Resort to them only in dire necessity.
Peace is our natural state of being.

If weapons must be wielded
to defend ourselves,

and we are victorious, never rejoice.
There is no joy in the slaughter of others.

On joyous occasions,
we attune with the yang side.
On sad occasions, with the yin.

During battle,
the soldiers are on the left yang side,
engaging in the combat.
The commanders are on the right yin side,
observing the action.

After the battle,
the soldiers who have slain others,
move to the yin side and mourn,
while the commanders,
now on the yang side,
are celebrating victory
even though it is a funeral.

## VERSE 31 COMMENTARY

Clearly, Lao Tzu stands opposed to war and all forms of aggression, but he condones defending oneself when attacked. However, even in the midst of self-defense, he calls for a consciousness that the use of weapons, the worst of all evils, is always a violation of our natural state of peacefulness. Furthermore, when we are victorious in defending ourselves from aggressors, this is no cause for rejoicing because we have violated our own humanity by killing others.

In Chinese medicine and philosophy the left side of the body is the yang or more active side while the right side is the yin or more nurturing side. The Chinese doctor palpates both the left and right radial arteries in different positions and depths as an important method of diagnosis. When a patient is healthy, it is normal for the left yang side to be a little stronger. Western medicine also observes the same differentiation, pointing out that the heart which pumps blood to all our arteries is located more on the left side of the chest cavity.

More recent observations of brain function differentiate the left side of the cerebral cortex as being more language and logic oriented, and so more capable of serving reasoning as well as rationalizing and manipulating roles. The right side of the cerebral cortex is identified as serving more intuitive, sensual and passive functions. Therefore, in Chinese terms, the left side of the brain is functionally more yang and the right side more yin. We are further reminded that there are some emotions that are more active and therefore relatively yang, such as celebrating joyous occasions, while other emotions are more passive and therefore more yin, such as sadness and grief.

Lao Tzu observes that during the battle, the soldier functions in a more yang way because he is the one engaging in combat. Therefore, he is metaphorically on the left yang side. On the other hand, the commanders, who are more likely to give the orders and stand back from the action, are thereby serving a more yin function. They are metaphorically on the right side.

Lastly, he provides the final paradoxical insight, observing that after the battle, their respective roles reverse. The soldiers, who have slain others, grieve for those whom they killed, thereby expressing their yin side, that is, their sadness. On the contrary, the commanders, who usually reap the credit for the victory, are prone to celebrate and be filled with their own ego satisfactions, a more yang expression.

# *Verse* 32

## IS IT NOT TIME TO UNIFY THE FRAGMENTS?

Although the Great Integrity is infinite,
and therefore undefined,
it is silent in its Primal Simplicity.

Nothing is its superior.
When humanity embraces
the Great Integrity,
all life on earth will be grateful.

All yin and yang will be harmonized
in the sweet daily dew,
and peace will reign on the planet
without anyone commanding it.

When the Primal Simplicity atomized
into the 10,000 fragments,
with their 10,000 names,
our planet became endangered.

Now – are there not enough fragments?
Is it not time to stop
and return to the universal sea
from which all streams emerged?

To return to the Great Integrity
is to obliterate
the list of the 10,000 endangered species.

## VERSE 32 COMMENTARY

In one sense, the ability to separate self from the environment began when our species became self-conscious. No other species on the planet has the ability to be aware of its own existence.

This estrangement took a qualitative leap when

communal tribal life gave way to civilizations, which pitted individuals and groups within society against each other. Thus the loss of the Great Integrity began in China about five thousand years ago, and Lao Tzu, who is said to have lived during the sixth century BCE, was already the product of more than two thousand years of fragmentation.

A third and higher level of fragmentation took place in modern times and led to the objectification expressed by the new mathematics of René Descartes, the new science of Isaac Newton, and the new form of human relations that looked on working people as a cost of production. This level was never experienced by Lao Tzu, but has been all too familiar to our generations of the past few hundred years.

Ten thousand is the number that the ancient Chinese used to signify the endless quantifications that all civilizations generate. Lao Tzu asks here, is it not time to stop fragmenting and return to our reunification with the universe represented by the Great Integrity? Although the loss of the Great Integrity in Lao Tzu's time threatened everyone's well being, it is not until our day that it has resulted in the extinction of thousands of species, and now also places our own species on the endangered list. My translation updates his question, placing it in the context of the new mega-madnesses of genocide, speciescide and even omnicide (the extinction of all life).

In Lao Tzu's time, the possibility of returning to the Great Integrity, that is, to a holistic life style and consciousness, was not realizable except spiritually, and even on this level it was attainable only by a few intellectuals like Lao Tzu whose full bellies, advanced consciousness, and relative independence, permitted what we might call a pseudo-holism. For the vast majority even pseudo-holism was an impossibility. As John Donne so succinctly pointed out, since no one is an island, entire by itself, when the bell tolls for one, it tolls for all. When liberation is not realizable by everyone, no one can completely return to the Great Integrity.

But today we are at that unique evolutionary stage when we can achieve an uncompromising integrity, when we can fulfill our human species capabilities, something that until now has been given to us only as a potential. Paradoxically, as Lao Tzu would point out if he were living today, we can now achieve the universal Great Integrity through those very ten thousand technologies that destroyed this integrity.

# *Verse* 33

## WHO ARE YOU?

If you understand others,
you are astute.
If you understand yourself,
you are insightful.

If you master others,
you are uncommonly forceful.
If you master yourself
you have uncommon inner strength.

If you know when you have enough,
you are wealthy.
If you carry your intentions to completion,
you are resolute.

If you find your roots and nourish them,
you will know longevity.
If you live a long creative life,
you will leave an eternal legacy.

## VERSE 33 COMMENTARY

In this verse, each couplet implies a comparative hierarchy of fulfillment. It is more fulfilling to understand yourself than to understand others. It is more fulfilling to have inner strength than to be forceful. It is more fulfilling to carry your intentions to completion than to know when you've had enough. And it is more fulfilling, not only for you, but also for all future generations, to live a long creative life rather than just a long one.

# *Verse* 34

## HUMILITY AND GREATNESS

The Great Integrity
is unboundable as a flood.
It cannot be manipulated this or that way.
It is the very wellspring of life,
always outpouring, never commanding.

Although the source for every need,
it is never demanding.
It does its work silently
and unpretentiously.

All return to the Great Integrity
as our liberating universal home.
By never seeking greatness,
greatness permeates in deed.

## VERSE 34 COMMENTARY

In other verses, Lao Tzu reminds us that our "normal" lives are so coercive that living in harmony with the Great Integrity seems impossible. How difficult it is, for example, to imagine receiving the most bountiful gifts without demanding them, or doing our work without announcing our successes, or experiencing greatness without seeking it. But, according to Lao Tzu, and to most leaders of the new consciousness and alternative social relations movements of our own time, we can return to the Great Integrity as our liberating universal home, and when we do, such behaviors will become our normal experience.

# Verse 35

## THE CONSUMMATE FOOD AND THE ULTIMATE MUSIC

When you merge with the universe,
the whole world is attracted to you,
discovering through you,
its own security, peace and good health.

Passing guests may stop by –
at first attracted to your savory food
and inspirational music.
But they might leave more deeply enriched
than they could have anticipated –

Because the silent song of Tao
is the ultimate music,
and the infinite delicacy of Tao
is the consummate nourishment.

## VERSE 35 COMMENTARY

Lao Tzu is no dualistic ascetic who deprecates the body and worships the soul. He doesn't preach that the ultimate peace is found only after death (provided, of course, that you have obeyed the commandments of your particular sect). On the contrary, his guests are attracted by his excellent food and music. However, when they leave, they may not only be sensually and alimentally satiated, but they might also become introduced to the wondrous experience of merging with the universal Great Integrity.

# Verse 36

## TOO MUCH INVITES DISASTER

What is overexpanded
becomes diminished.
What is too strong becomes weakened.
What is too high is cut down.
What is overpossessed
becomes impoverished.

It is in the nature of process
that in the final stages,
those who are overextended,
overarmed and overprivileged,
shall be overcome.

Disaster stalks the fish
which swims up from its deep water home,
and the army which threatens to conquer
those beyond its own borders.

## VERSE 36 COMMENTARY

My translation of this verse expresses what Lao Tzu could only imply. If he were as openly rebellious in his language as expressed in the translation, he might never have reached the more than ninety years he was supposed to have lived!

Specifically, while my last line cautions about armies being used to conquer others, Lao Tzu's words are more literally: *A nation's weapons should be shown to no one.*

Similarly, the metaphors Lao Tzu uses as arguments for his conclusion only imply the issue of overabundance and overprivilege. The more literal translation of Lao Tzu's first two lines is:

> If one wants to diminish, one must first expand.
> If one wants to weaken, one must first strengthen.

However, the process of diminishing does not necessarily follow any expansion, but requires overexpansion. The process of weakening does not necessarily follow strengthening but requires overstrengthening or overarming. It is only the excess condition that produces its opposite.

# *Verse* 37

## THE PRIMAL SIMPLICITY

The Great Integrity imposes no action,
yet it leaves nothing undone.
Were governments to embrace it,
everything would develop naturally.

If thereafter an old ego should reincarnate,
the already permeated Primal Simplicity
would neutralize it in its pervasive silence.

Returning to silence is returning to peace.
Returning to peace,
the world reharmonizes itself.

物將自化：而欲作吾將鎮之以無名之樸無
名之樸亦將不欲不欲以靜天下將自正

## VERSE 37 COMMENTARY

When the great transformation of our planet takes place, and we return to the Great Integrity, that doesn't mean that all the old habits will automatically disappear forever. It is likely that old egos will reincarnate for a while. However, once the new social condition permeates widely and deeply enough, we should expect that these old aberrations will tend to be more and more readily neutralized by a more and more widely and deeply pervading milieu of peace and harmony.

# *Verse* 38

## DISTINGUISHING THE HIGHEST FROM THE LOWEST MORALITY

You can readily recognize
the highest virtuousness
because it never places itself on display.
You can readily recognize
the lowest virtuousness
because it is always announcing itself.

The highest virtue
quietly serves universal needs.
The lowest virtue
actively strives for personal success.
The highest morality serves common needs.
The lowest morality is self-serving.

True benevolence
acts without intention.
But when rituals go unheeded,
they are enforced with rolled-up sleeves.

Failing the Great Integrity,
we resort to virtuousness.
Failing virtuousness,
we resort to moralizing.
Failing moralizing, we resort to dogma,
the most superficial form
of faith and loyalty,
and the nourishment for confusion.

Natural persons are attracted
to substance rather than form,
to the nutritious fruit
rather than the enticing flower,
to that which dwells deeply within,
rather than to that which clings
superficially to the surface.

## VERSE 38 COMMENTARY

The highest forms of morality are directed to serving the needs of others, and are carried out quietly, with humility and without self-conscious intention.

The lowest forms are precisely the opposite. They are motivated by ego satisfactions, fulfilling personal self-interests, and by announcing their own beneficence.

Four specific levels of integrity are differentiated from the highest level: the Great Integrity, to the lowest level: the coercive enforcement of dogma and ritual. In between are virtuousness and moralizing that are middle grounds between the highest and lowest moralities.

It is interesting to note that Lao Tzu had nothing but contempt for ritual, while for Confucius, his younger contemporary, ritual was the pinnacle of virtue. How ironic that, according to legend, Confucius went to visit Lao Tzu to become enlightened on matters of ritual since Lao Tzu held the position of archivist for the State of Chu. Needless to say, Confucius stormed out of his audience with Lao Tzu denouncing him as a dangerous dragon! Soon after this incident, it is said that Lao Tzu – only in mid-life – retired from his official position and fled to the mountains to live the rest of his life in seclusion.

# *Verse* 39

## THEN AND NOW

In ancient times, all entities
had their own integrity and function.
The sky was clear and endless.
The earth was calm and firm.
The gods were charged
with spiritual powers.
The wells were clean and full.
The 10,000 creatures
were healthy and fecund.
Leaders were elected to plan the work
and defense of the community.
How wondrously concordant!

If the sky were not endless,
it could have fallen.
If the earth were not firm,
it could have burst.

If the gods did not exercise
their spiritual powers,
they would have been abandoned.
If the wells were not full,
they could have dried up.
If the 10,000 creatures
were not productive,
they could have become extinct.
If the leaders did not plan the work
and defense of the community,
they would have been replaced.
In this way, each entity
had its own essentiality,
each part complementing every other.

Nowadays, when the privileged among us
identify themselves with the orphan,
the widower and the hungry one,
it may be an opportunistic appeal
for the support of the lowly,
or a realization that loudly trumpeting
self-glory negates itself,

or a premonition that shining like jade,
and resounding like stone chimes
attracts the desperate adventurers
among those deprived of hope,
inviting disaster among those
who create these deprivations.

## VERSE 39 COMMENTARY

In ancient times, when all lived as part of the Great Integrity, each had its own function, performing it with integrity and with respect for all other entities. When one did not fulfill its function, it was replaced for the good of all, because poor functioning of one entity threatened all others.

Nowadays, (from even before the time of Lao Tzu right through our own day), the privileged tend to care only for their own well-being, while the under-privileged are deprived of realizing their capabilities and of benefiting from the bountifulness of all the available resources. The former, having for the most part lost their moral integrity, tend to rationalize these inequities in the ten thousand opportunistic masquerades, some of which Lao Tzu lists in the final stanza.

# *Verse 40*

## ALL IS PARADOX

The movement of the Great Integrity
is infinite,
yet its character is passive.
Being defines every form of life,
yet all originate in,
and return to, non-being.

### VERSE 40 COMMENTARY

The "Old Wise Man" never tires of reminding us that our senses and our logic are more illusion than reality. Wisdom, he says, derives rather from paradox, which in turn derives from the contradictions in our observations and conclusions, as well as from the very nature of transformation, which is itself, the defining character of the universe.

What is the nature of transformation? It is the tendency for everything when it becomes extreme to turn into its opposite. When we are overactive (extreme yang in Chinese terms) we must rest or sleep (yin) or else we will not survive. When we stay outside in very cold weather for a long time (extreme yin) we must find some source of heat (yang) or else we might die.

The main application of paradox and the principle of opposites for us today is that having reached the point in the development of modern civilization of extreme violence, competitiveness and fragmentation (extreme yang) we are now seeding the transformation to its opposite: Lao Tzu's Great Integrity (yin). Here is a key to our closet of lost hopes. Indeed, we have been appointed by evolution to become the conscious agents of our own transcendence.

Clearly, in order to accommodate us to continue to participate in a now anachronistic competitive ego-driven world of *haves* at war with the *have-nots*, we are asked to accept our social condition and its rationalizations as the only one possible and desirable in this "best of all possible worlds". (Voltaire) The spirit of Lao Tzu has reincarnated, inviting us to laugh at these mythologies that serve only the selfish interests of the over-privileged. He reminds us again and again that movement, not statics and paradox, not logic, is the nature of reality.

# Verse 41

## OBSERVING AND NOURISHING PARADOX

When most people
hear about the Great Integrity,
they waiver between belief and disbelief.
When wise people
hear about the Great Integrity,
they diligently follow its path.
When ignorant people hear about it
they laugh out loud!
By this very laughter,
we know its authenticity.

It is said that –
enlightenment appears dark,
the progressive way appears retrograde,
the smooth way appears jagged,

the highest peak of revelation
appears empty like a valley,
the cleanest appears to be soiled,
the greatest abundance
appears insufficient,
the most enduring inner strength
appears like weakness,
and creativity appears imitative.

Great talents mature slowly.
Great sounds are silent.
Great forms look shapeless.
Transcendent squareness has no corners.

The Great Integrity hides behind all forms,
stubbornly nourishing the paradoxes
that can enlighten us.

## VERSE 41 COMMENTARY

One of the important differentiations between the thought structures of Lao Tzu and of conventional science is the metaphoric-paradoxic character of the former and the objective and logical character of the latter. To Lao Tzu, contradictions often reveal a deep truth. To modern science, contradictions indicate an error. This verse is saturated with the paradoxes that surface when one experiences life through the Great Integrity, that is, through our intuitive holistic consciousness.

It is the left cerebral hemisphere that formulates logical alienated thinking, which requires the modern conventional scientist to separate himself from that which he is investigating.

In contrast, the Great Integrity is a holistic consciousness, which predominantly activates the right cerebral hemisphere and is both phylogenetically and ontogenetically an earlier mode of perception. Right-brain dominance was characteristic of the first few million years that hominids wandered through our planet. It is also the only form of perception of every one of us during our infancy and the dominant form during our prelogical early childhood years.

According to Lao Tzu and to many of us who are exploring a more appropriate consciousness for the twenty-first century, a new Great Integrity will transcend our present objective consciousness. My view of evolutionary transformation proposes that this new Great Integrity will not be a return to right hemispheric dominance, but to a new left-right hemispheric merger in which both our thoughts and feelings, our objective apperceptions and subjective perceptions, will function as a higher level of integral human exchange. Such a development assumes a new mode of communication that will be objective and scientific (like language) as well as subjective and feelingful (like music), but without the duality that now characterizes their relationship. The new music-language might also permit the communication of simultaneous multiplicities, especially involving the processes of transformation. Until now, the limitations inherent in the linearity of our thinking and of our languages have required us to communicate the complexities of our experiences by analyzing and presenting them in sequential fragments like the frame-by-frame photographs in a cinema.

# Verse 42

## THE PRINCIPLES OF TRANSFORMATION

The Great Integrity expresses one.
One manifests as two.
Two is transformed into three.
And three generates all the myriad entities
of the universe.

Every entity always returns to yin
after engaging yang.
The fusion of these two opposites
births the Vital Energy
that sustains the harmony of life.

But for most people,
this harmony is decimated
by inheriting a condition
of, misery and victimization.

Politicians cleverly pretend
that they too originate
from the toxic soil of this misery,
even while designing the very laws
that legitimate victimization.

But watch out –
those who hoard oversufficiency
will be diminished!
And those who are diminished
will become bountiful!

These commonly known truths
that common people
teach each other,
are also my truths.

As you sow,
so shall you reap.
Such is the heart of my teaching
in a world forced to live heartlessly.

## VERSE 42 COMMENTARY

This verse summarizes the origin and theory of the Great Integrity (*Tao*) its practice (*Te*), its violations, and the teachings that can function as guides (*Ching*) to return us to a holistic and integral life (*Tao*). The evolution of the Great Integrity is summarized in the first short stanza which encapsulates the intuitive wisdom of the ancients, and which is now validated by the latest scientific theories.

Specifically, this evolution is postulated as being rooted in the great underlining truth of the universe as expressing the metaphor of *one*. We can now in the twenty-first century translate that metaphor as a recognition that every entity in the universe is related to and inherent in every other part. In the early 1970s, I discovered that the ancient Chinese Vital Energy (Qi or Ch'i) system of acupoints and channels is reiterated in each part of the body, and furthermore, that each of these anatomical parts manifests acupoints to the rest of the body that are hologrammatic to the anatomy of the body. I called these *micro-acupuncture systems*. Karl Pribram discovered that the brain was also holonomic, and that each part of the brain, contained the knowledge of the whole brain. Microbiologists (Sivik and Schoenfeld) have discovered that "in every single cell of every human organism, the sum total of the whole life experience of every living organism since the beginning of time is preserved". David Bohm, a colleague of Albert Einstein, applied the holonomic concept to the nature of the entire universe. All of these investigations translate Lao Tzu's intuitive concept of the Great Integrity in scientific terms.

The Great Integrity manifests as *two* through the universality of opposites: passive and active, cold and hot, wet and dry, slow and fast, low and high, negative and positive – all of which are categorized by the ancient Chinese as yin and yang.

Since the time of Hegel (1770–1831), modern dialectics has shown how the *two* is transformed into *three*. Hegel reveals how everything in the universe is always involved in transformation, and that every process involves the conflict of opposites (yin and yang, thesis and antithesis), which resolves into a third entity (synthesis).

# *Verse* 43

## THE VALUE OF MINIMUMS

That which is most tender
can overcome that which is most rigid.
That which has least substance
can penetrate that which has least space.

Acting without deliberate action,
and teaching without uttering a word
are rarely practiced.
So few find their way
to the Great Integrity!

## VERSE 43 COMMENTARY

天下之至柔馳騁天下之至堅無有入於無間吾是以知無為之有益不言之教無為之益天下希及之

Most of us become addicted to maximums – maximum possessions, maximum power, maximum praise, and maximum leisure.

Although they are toxic, they function as compulsive compensations for our inability to fulfill our human needs. Lao Tzu sings the praises of minimums inviting us to appreciate their higher value. Nevertheless, he never expresses blame or guilt when we choose the maximums instead. He only observes that most of us are by and large making poor choices. He probably sensed that higher alternative values cannot resonate widely until we all grow up in families and communities that nurture these values.

# *Verse* 44

## CHOICES

Which do you value more –
your wealth or your wellness?
Which is more harmful –
to lead or to lose?

The greater is your attachment,
the more bereft is your release.
The more you hoard,
the less is left to enjoy.

Those on the path
to the Great Integrity
flow without forcing,
leaving no space for disasters.

名與身孰親身與貨孰多得與亡孰病是故
甚愛必大費多藏必厚亡知足不辱知止不
殆可以長久

## VERSE 44 COMMENTARY

Most people, given the opportunity, would choose wealth over wellness, winning over losing. They cling desperately and dependently in their close relationships, and hoard their possessions. These are choices, says Lao Tzu, that lead to disaster. Our alternative is to flow without forcing, and to release ourselves from our false values and counter-productive behaviors. Like *Verse 43*, it is useful to be reminded of the choices and values that can help to direct us toward the path leading to the Great Integrity, but to stay the course, people from everywhere need to join us.

# Verse 45

## ILLUSION AND REALITY

Completeness can seem incomplete,
yet the completeness that we achieve
can be remarkable.
Fullness can seem empty,
yet the fullness that we achieve
can be very useful.

Truth can appear as lie.
Straightness can appear as twisted.
Skillfulness can appear to be clumsy.
Eloquence can sound like foolishness.

But the dialectic of yin and yang
is not illusory.
Activity can overcome cold.
Tranquillity can overcome heat.
And peacefulness is the natural seed
of a violent world.

## VERSE 45 COMMENTARY

大成若缺其用不敝大盈若沖其用不窮大
直若屈大巧若拙大辯若訥躁勝寒靜勝
熱清靜為天下正

We live in a world of illusions, but not all is illusory. We live in a world of realities, but not all is real. That which is most illusory is our belief that everything must be either complete or incomplete, full or empty, straight or crooked, skillful or clumsy, eloquent or not. That which is most real is the experience of process, for example, of activity overcoming cold or of tranquillity overcoming heat.

In all processes, when one extreme is reached, its opposite is ripe to generate. The most significant potential process of our time is the re-establishment of the Great Integrity. Why? It is because extreme fragmentation, violence and cruelty have now become so prevalent.

# *Verse* 46

## ENOUGH IS ENOUGH!

When the Great Integrity
permeated our lives,
freely galloping horses fertilized the fields.

When the Great Integrity was lost,
war horses were bred in the countryside.

There is no greater calamity
than acquisitiveness racing out of control.

Only those who know
when enough is enough
can ever have enough.

## VERSE 46 COMMENTARY

天下有道卻走馬以糞天下無道戎馬生於
郊罪莫大於可欲禍莫大於不知足咎莫大
於欲得故知足之足常足矣

There is no greater loss than that of the Great Integrity. Since we have exchanged it for the curse of greed, we have inherited all manner of social calamities. Our insatiable desires for possessions, and our compensatory psyches binging to feed our starving egos, have bred a perverted consciousness to navigate a perverted world. Rebirthing our world as a cooperating global village, and rebirthing our consciousness as the Great Integrity, can recreate our awareness of when enough is enough. Only then will we be released from the omnipresent prisons of selfishness in which we have all been trapped during this temporary five thousand-year era of civilizations as we have known them.

# *Verse* 47

## GOING BEYOND

We can understand the world
as it is without leaving our home.
We can understand the world
as it might be
without peering dreamily out our window.

The further we go,
the less we know.

Wise people understand the 10,000 things
without going to each one.
They know them
without having to look at each one,
and they transform all
without acting on each one.

## VERSE 47 COMMENTARY

Since our main problem in life is transcending our inherited pathological institutions and their rationales, it is counterproductive to immerse ourselves in all their perverted details. We don't have to experience every toxic habit and premise. To transcend our present way of life requires our creating alternative ways of relating to each other and new holistic ways of thinking. Endlessly traveling all the old roads and peering through all the old windows will tend only to lock us more tightly into our past.

Another implication of this verse is the need to release ourselves from the naïve illusions of pragmatism. These illusions urge us to rely upon our direct experience as the basis for our premises, conclusions and actions. Lao Tzu has no trust in understandings that come solely out of our perceptions, or out of coercive actions that derive from our desires – however well-observed are the perceptions, and however well-intentioned are the actions.

# *Verse 48*

## ALL IS DONE WITHOUT DOING

To obtain a diploma
requires the storage of trivia.
To obtain the Great Integrity
requires their abandonment.

The more we are released
from vested fragments of knowledge,
the less we are compelled
to take vested actions,
until all is done without doing.

When the ego interferes
in the rhythms of process,
there is so much doing!
But nothing is done.

## VERSE 48 COMMENTARY

Is Lao Tzu stuck in a literary mannerism involving paradox? Or is there a deep insight into the concept of "all is done without doing", a repeated premise in many of these eighty-one verses?

What Lao Tzu means by "doing" is acting against the rhythms of natural processes and against the pretended natural inertia and laziness of human beings, to make something happen. That means that "doing" implies actions impelled by interference, force and coercion. Such actions are always in opposition to natural processes, and usually in violation of human needs and well-being.

What Lao Tzu means by "getting done" is to flow with and facilitate natural processes, and never violate the needs and harmony of human beings in the process of producing the needs of the community. "Getting done" is always cooperating with nature and with other people. "Doing" is always a violation of nature and the exploitation of other people.

Therefore what he means by "all is done without doing" is that everything is accomplished without coercion.

What Lao Tzu is always concerned with is the re-establishment of the Great Integrity. For him, the Great Integrity is the return to intuition and the merging of self and non-self. For us, having evolved to a different stage of evolution, we don't want to throw away our hundreds of years of scientific experience. For us, our return to the Great Integrity means an integrity at a much higher level than Lao Tzu could imagine. Our Great Integrity is to integrate our now advanced scientific left brain with our intuitive artistic right brain. For us, returning to the Great Integrity is to end our schizoid patterns of acting and thinking by establishing a planetary community in which cooperation replaces competition, war between countries becomes an anachronism because there will be no separate countries, and where all the fragmentations and coercive acts of the past will be exchanged for a Great Integrity beyond the wildest dreams of Lao Tzu.

# *Verse* 49

## WISDOM

Wise people are not absorbed
in their own needs.
They take the needs of all people
as their own.

They are good to the good.
But they are also good
to those who are still absorbed
in their own needs.

Why?
Because goodness is in the very nature
of the Great Integrity.

Wise people trust those who trust.
But they also trust those who do not trust.

Why?
Because trusting is in the very nature
of the Great Integrity.

Wise people merge with all others
rather than stand apart judgmentally.
In this way,
all begin to open their ears and hearts,
more prepared
to return to the innocence of childhood.

## VERSE 49 COMMENTARY

One premise here is that wisdom and humanity require the ability to subordinate one's own ego demands, personal needs and predilections in order to identify with the needs of all people.

A second implied premise is that no matter how each of us may in some ways become corrupted by social demands, bribes and indoctrinations, there is an innate humanity somewhere in the core of every human being.

A third implied premise is that by addressing this

human Essence in each person, we prevent ourselves from becoming cynics, and allow those of us who have become corrupted to return to our essential human nature, that is, to the innocence of our childhood.

# Verse 50

## THE FORCES OF LIFE AND DEATH

Every one of us is born,
and everyone dies.

However, three of every ten
seem to be born to live,
three seem to be born to die,
and three live lifefully or deathfully
according to their chosen life styles.

But only one in ten
seems to survive all dangers.
When walking through the jungle,
this one never fears the rhinoceros
because there seems to be
no place in her to butt his horns.

She never fears the tiger
because there seems to be
no place to sink his claws.
And she never fears weapons
because there seems to be
no place their steel can penetrate.

This is the fulfilled person
of the Great Integrity
who leaves no space in life
for premature death.

## VERSE 50 COMMENTARY

Chinese medicine identifies two main sources of Vital Energy (*Qi*) that determine our ability to survive adversity. The first is called *Yuan* or *Genetic Qi*. It is the Vital Energy we inherit from our parents. The second is called *Hou Tian Zhi* or *Acquired Qi*. It is the Vital Energy that derives from our life style, that is, from the air we breathe, the food and drink we ingest, our exposure to the sun and its full spectrum light, our actions and emotions through which we relate to others and to our environment, and the people and their Qi with whom we most directly intersect.

Four kinds of people are differentiated here according to their life force which protects them, or their death force which threatens them.

(1) Those who seem to have been "born to live". These are the three of every ten people who Lao Tzu identifies as having inherited a strong Yuan Qi from their parents.

(2) Those who seem to have been "born to die" because they seem not to have "selected" their parents so wisely.

(3) Those whose choice of life style determines whether they live "lifefully" or "deathfully". Those who lead a life style that supports their Vital Energy thereby facilitate their own health and longevity, while those who lead a life style that challenges and insults their Vital Energy weaken their health and invite an early death.

(4) Lastly, are those who seem to be impervious to harm and premature death because they live in harmony

with others, with the universe and with themselves. This, of course is living in the Great Integrity. Today, although we might be fortunate in inheriting a strong genetic Qi, and we might choose our life styles relatively wisely, we cannot live entirely in the Great Integrity because our social environment is more or less a contradiction of the Great Integrity. This contradiction is manifested in most of our institutions, whether family, work, religion, schooling, sports, leisure, politics, economics, medical care, or whatever. Since we are all social beings and cannot avoid growing up in the womb of these predominantly corrupt institutions, the nearest we can come to living the Great Integrity is by rejecting many of their values, premises and behaviors. Instead, we can follow Lao Tzu's alternative consciousness, transforming our own personal lives as we participate in the transformation of our institutions. It is only after we succeed in attaining these goals that any of us will be "walking the waters", never fearing that weapons will harm us, because there will be no harmful weapons in a planet that embraces the Great Integrity.

# *Verse* 51

## NATURAL BIRTHING

All in the universe
derive from the Primal Integrity.
The interaction of yin and yang
shapes and nourishes them,
and evolution ever transforms them
in their endless ecological dance.

Therefore, in its own way,
every entity celebrates its Primal Mother.
Not out of any mandate.
Not out of any obligation.
But solely as the expression
of its own integrity.

## VERSE 51 COMMENTARY

The way of the Tao – the great, undifferentiated universe and Mother of all entities – is natural, spontaneous and unconscious. Contrary to current human relationships, this Great Integrity is not acknowledged by mandate or obligation, but only as an "is-ness". This verse, thereby refers to the integrity of all life including us human beings before we left our metaphoric "Garden of Eden" that we shared with all other life on the planet. We were separated from the universal "Garden" by acquiring knowledge, that is, self-consciousness, differentiating ourselves from all that is *Not-Us*.

By excluding us civilized human beings in this verse, we are reminded how natural and universal is the Great Integrity when you remove us from the picture.

Only we modern homo sapiens traded the Great Integrity for its opposite: the Great Alienation, which has resulted in our victimizing nature, each other, and of course, ourselves. It is only we who have brought misery into the world as a product of selling our Integrity to the metaphoric devil who is the incarnation of every form of fragmentation.

The question that Lao Tzu never does raise, because each generation asks only the questions it is capable of solving, is: now that we humans have lost the Great Integrity and thereby created gross ugliness and suffering, and more recently, even the capability of destroying most life on this once thriving planet, what is to be done? How can we neutralize our own satanic power? Lao Tzu has no strategic answer. But we do. It is to rewrite and live Lao Tzu's *Theory and Practice of the Great Integrity*. Unless we do, there might not be any recovery of the Great Integrity or any twenty-second century for us.

# Verse 52

## RETURNING TO OUR ORIGINS

Everything has a common origin
that we might call
the Mother of the Universe.

Once in pre-conscious times,
we were all a part of this Mother,
just as we – all her children –
were part of each other.

This was when we were all
umbilically still attached
to the Great Integrity.

Some thousands of years ago,
our species alone

issued a declaration of independence
from our Mother.
Now it is time to reunite with her.

Thereafter, we will never any more suffer
the 10,000 miseries
that only we human beings have acquired.

Block all the loopholes!
Shut all the doors to the old temptations!
And we will never again feel deprived.

If we crawl through the loopholes,
if we race through the gate
back to the 10,000 addictions,
we will never be fulfilled.

How shall we know the Great Integrity?
When our insights proliferate
even in the smallest matters.
When our strength is boundless
even while ever yielding.

We can keep our outsights
when returning to our insights.
In this way, we will reharmonize
with our Mother,
celebrating the Great Integrity
on a higher level.

## VERSE 52 COMMENTARY

In the beginning was the wordless unity of every entity with Mother Nature.

Billions of years and millions of species later came the innocent word generated in the social-body-minds of our hominid ancestors.

Several millions of years still later, with the advent of civilizations as we have known them, came the coercive word which rationalized the inequities that history has called "progress".

This progress might now be defined as an incredibly advanced technology. It is a great paradox that it is this very technology, although we sacrificed our humanity for it, that might provide us with one of the main prerequisites for planetary abundance, peace, and community, and thereby the recovery of our lost humanity.

The last stanza proposes that if we keep our *outsights* (the knowledge we have accumulated from our scientific and technological discoveries) when we return to our *insights* (our reharmonization with each other, with nature and with ourselves), we will celebrate the Great Integrity on a higher level than any species in the entire evolution of life on this planet, even though our species was the only one that ever lost it.

# *Verse* 53

## NOT YET ON THE WAY

Those who have the smallest grain
of wisdom
would want to walk
the simple path
of the Great Integrity.
Their only fear would be to go astray.

Indeed, there is a good reason to fear
when most of the world
is piled into two wagons
racing toward each other
on a single lane road.

In one over-crowded wagon
is the vast majority
who live in weedy fields
with empty granaries.

In the other wagon
are those whose garments
are opulently embroidered.
They gorge themselves on rich foods
far beyond their appetites,
and guzzle inebriating drinks
far beyond their thirst.

They accumulate wealth
even beyond their avaricious cravings
while armed to the teeth
against their starving neighbors.

Surely such thievish degradation
couldn't be the way
to the Great Integration!

## VERSE 53 COMMENTARY

What could be more in contradiction to the Great Integrity than our civilizations, which for the past few thousand years have been divided into the over-privileged, and the underprivileged, with these inequities maintained by armed police, courts and prisons called our system of "justice".

The last line which acknowledges the impossibility of such a depraved way of life ever leading to the Great Integrity is rhymed out of deference to the original which makes a pun of the word *tao* which is both the Chinese word for the *Great Integrity* as well as the word for *thievery*, with both meanings of *tao* utilizing the same intonation (the fourth tone).

# *Verse* 54

## THE WHOLE IS IN EACH PART

Whatever is planted deeply
is not easily uprooted.
Whatever is embraced sincerely
does not crave escape.
Ever since we lost our intuition
as our main guide in life,
these virtues have had to be
consciously cultivated to survive.

Cultivate them in yourself
and they will be genuine.
Cultivate them in your family
and they will surely flourish.
Cultivate them in your community
and they will be long lasting.

Cultivate them in your country
and they will be widely propagated.
Cultivate them in the world
and they will certainly become universal.

In this way you will know others
by what you do yourself.
You will know families
by what you contribute as a family.
You will know the world
by what you do as a planetary citizen.

How do we know all this?
Because we know
that each part is the whole,
and the whole is in each part.

## VERSE 54 COMMENTARY

There are three main insights that Lao Tzu shares with us in this verse:

(1) That once we all practiced the Great Integrity. This was in prehistoric times when we were one with nature and each other.

(2) That now that we have lost our intuition as our main guide to decision-making, the only way we can re-establish our integrity is through the conscious cultivation of alternative behaviors.

(3) That if we are to acquire a truly holistic consciousness, it cannot be done only through self-enlightenment, or only by creating a more democratic political structure. We must transform and transcend at every level – as individuals, as families, as communities and as a planetary village. The further implication here is that there is no sequential formula that will work. That is, individual enlightenment will not, by itself, lead to planetary community, nor will institutional change, by itself, lead to our transformation from selfish to integral personalities. All levels of transformation must evolute in tandem *because we know that each part is the whole and the whole is in each part.*

# *Verse* 55

## THE PROMISES OF THE GREAT INTEGRITY

When we will live in complete integrity
we will be innocent like newborn babies.
Wasps and scorpions will not sting us.
Wild beasts will not maul us.
Birds of prey will not seize us.

Our bones will be pliable,
our sinews soft.
Yet our grip will be firm.
Even before we have known conjugality,
our sexuality will be easily aroused
because we will be so virile.

We'll sing all day long
without becoming hoarse
because we'll be in full harmony.

To be in harmony
is to live in the Great Integrity,
the ultimate wisdom.

However, to interfere with nature
is to seek control.
To seek control is to create *dis-stress*.
To create *dis-stress* produces exhaustion.
All these negations of the Great Integrity
also negate life and its longevity.

## VERSE 55 COMMENTARY

Living in the Great Integrity is living in harmony with nature, with each other and with ourselves. This harmony defines an integrity that will allow us to transcend both our self-imposed antagonisms with nature as well as the present limitations of our physical, sexual, artistic, intellectual and spiritual capacities. However, when we coerce nature, each other and ourselves, we create *dis-stress*, exhaustion, illness, and death.

# *Verse* 56

## HOW TO PREPARE FOR THE GREAT INTEGRITY

Those who know don't lecture.
Those who lecture don't know.

To prepare the way for the Great Integrity –
Close the rationalizing routes!
Shut the gloomy gates!
Blunt the sharp edges!
Release those who are tethered!
Soften the blinding lights!
Unite the world!

We cannot achieve the Great Integrity
through intimacy or emotional detachment,
nor through posturing or humility.

Since the Great Integrity
makes no judgments or demands,
how will we know when it has arrived?
When it permeates us
with its universal "is-ness".

## VERSE 56 COMMENTARY

How do we prepare the way for the Great Integrity? Certainly not through lecturing, because "those who lecture don't know". Then how?

By giving up rationalizing, by laughing, by eliminating our sharp antagonisms, by re-educating and releasing those who are imprisoned, by burying blame and revenge, and by giving up our coercive relations.

Lao Tzu reminds us that we cannot achieve the Great Integrity through either intimacy or detachment, nor through force or humility.

And how will we know when it has arrived? *When it permeates us with its universal "is-ness".*

# *Verse* 57

## SIMPLICITY BLOSSOMS WHEN COERCION DIES

Govern a state with predictable actions.
Fight a war with surprise attacks.
But the universe becomes ours
only by eliminating coercive acts.
By not doing, nothing lacks.

How do we know these lessons?
By tuning into our Essence.

The more prohibitions there are,
the poorer the people become.
The more deadly weapons there are,
the more our fears turn us numb.

When craftiness spreads far,
the more bizarre what is done,
The stricter the laws there are,
the less the robbers run.

Therefore, the wise know
to make no one a foe.
The less coercing we do,
The more tranquillities grow.

When harmony reigns,
and we rule ourselves with felicity,
everyone gains,
and we'll all live in simplicity.

以正治國以奇用兵以無事取天下吾何以知其
然哉以此天下多忌諱而民彌貧民多利器國
家滋昏人多伎巧奇物滋起法令滋彰盜賊
多有故聖人云我無為而民自化我好靜而民
自正我無事而民自富我無欲而民自樸我
無情而民自清

## VERSE 57 COMMENTARY

There is a popular saying that money is the root of all evil. That's a cover-up. The real root of evil is coercion. Money is the bribe that enforces inequitable exchanges. When bribes are insufficient, then brute force becomes the *modus vivendi*.

If coercion is the enemy, then cooperation is the liberator. When coercion dies, the Great Integrity is reborn. *When harmony reigns, and we rule ourselves with felicity, everyone gains, and we'll all live in simplicity.*

# Verse 58

## ALTERNATIVES

When a government is more benign,
the people are more productive.
When a government is more tyrannical,
the people are more rebellious.

But whatever the government,
if disaster is the bitter fruit
of others' good fortune,
how long
can such injustice be tolerated?
How long
we have endured the hypocrisies!

Those pretending to be righteous
act deceitfully.

Those pretending to be religious
revert to evil.
We have been deluded!
And each day it becomes worse!

Be firm and armed, but do no harm!
Be as sharp as a knife, but do not cut!
Be ready to transform, but do not provoke!
Illuminate the darkness of ignorance,
but do not blind!

## VERSE 58 COMMENTARY

Even in Lao Tzu's time, the impoverishment of some people was the source of others' good fortune. These injustices, he says, were rationalized by deceits which have deluded the people for so long

What shall we do? Lao Tzu's advice in the last stanza is still sound. We need to be firm, clear and prepared to transform our lives, but the process should be one without arrogance or provocation, never victimizing others as we have been victimized.

# *Verse* 59

## THE IMPORTANCE OF MODERATION

To serve humanity,
there is nothing more important
than to be moderate.

To be moderate Verse 58
is to return to the female yin principle.

To return to the yin
is to become nurturing.

To be nurturing
is to acquire enormous capacity.

To have enormous capacity
is to be ready for the Great Integrity.

To be ready for the Great Integrity
is to be ready to serve humanity.

In this way we will become firmly planted
in the Great Integrity,
the pathway to a clear vision
and a long life.

## VERSE 59 COMMENTARY

This verse is all about the synergy of our visions for the future and our present life styles. The Great Integrity is a universal nurturing of our common identity, that is, the predominance of the yin cooperating harmony of all entities. How do we ready ourselves for the Great Integrity? By practicing moderation and nurturing peace, love and integrity in our hearts, dreams and everyday lives.

# *Verse* 60

## OUR FUTURE

Govern a country
like you would fry a small fish –
with care, respect
and with the least interference.

When the world is governed
according to the Great Integrity,
evil will lose its power.

Not only will evil lose its power,
it will no longer even exist.

When evil ceases to exist,
neither will good exist.

Without good and evil,
we simply will live totally
in our human natures.

No one will compromise anyone else
because we will all be
inextricable parts of the Great Integrity.

## VERSE 60 COMMENTARY

Governing a large country with the tender care that is needed to fry a small fish is a preparation of our minds, hearts and behaviors to live in the Great Integrity.

When we achieve the Great Integrity, there will be no separate countries and no politicians to rule over us. Nor will there be coercive behaviors and institutions that force us to live inequitably.

When *evil* no longer exists, its opposite, *good*, also ceases to have any meaning. Therefore, when we finally re-establish the Great Integrity, we human beings will live without good and evil, just as every other species on our planet. Instead, we will simply be liberated to express our human natures in all our thoughts, feelings and activities.

# Verse 61

## A PLEA FOR MUTUAL HUMILITY

In our era when the Great Integrity
has been lost,
separate states have arisen.
Some become very large.
Others remain very small.

When the larger ones
try to conquer the small,
at first the smaller ones are defeated
even though yang aggression
meets yang resistance.
But death stalks the people
on both sides of war.

Is it not better for great countries to be
like vast low lying lands
into which all streams passively go?

And the smaller countries,
like the innocent streams,
can be welcomed
at the end of their passage
by wide open arms,
calmly receiving their flow?

Would not this mutual humility
save countless lives now,
while serving as a rehearsal
for the coming of the Tao?

## VERSE 61 COMMENTARY

From the time of Lao Tzu to our own day, our planet has been carved up by superpowers that have subjugated smaller countries to serve their own selfish needs. Today, superpowers are anachronistic. Just as hominid hordes evolved into clans, and clans evolved into tribes, and tribes into city-states, and city-states into countries, our time is the evolutionary moment for countries to dissolve into a single planetary community expressing the Great Integrity.

In Lao Tzu's time such an evolutionary step was only a utopian wish that could not yet be realized. So here in this verse the great ancient wise man shares his dreams, providing idealistic alternatives that he must have known could not be realized in his time. Because we are the first generations that can put these dreams into practice, how much more intensively and realistically do Lao Tzu's words echo in our ears, minds and hearts than they did for Lao Tzu's own contemporaries?

It is obvious that globalization defines the evolutionary stage of our twenty-first century. The question that has not been resolved is whose globalization will it be? That which will serve transnational, international and superpower hegemonies? Or a global village where the Great Integrity will at last fulfill the hearts and dreams of all humanity and the needs of our universal Mother – the Great Ecology that defines and embraces all life on our planet?

# *Verse* 62

## REHEARSALS FOR THE GREAT INTEGRITY

The Great Integrity is the sanctuary
of all human beings.

For those who are honest and caring,
it is a guide and a treasure.

For those who are dishonest and deceitful,
it is also a treasure because a good word
can rationalize a selfish act,
and because a good act, now and then,
can serve as a mask
for living extravagantly
from the misery of others.

Since the Great Integrity
is so universally acknowledged,

don't cast away
those who use it opportunistically.
Rather cast away the opportunities
to live selfishly so that the Great Integrity
can more fully permeate all our lives.

We might begin with the inauguration
ceremonies of our leaders.
Instead of showering them
with precious gifts,
instead of the public swearing
of meaningless oaths,
why not share a meditation
on the Great Integrity as a prelude
to its comprehensive embrace?

## VERSE 62 COMMENTARY

The main premise here is that no human being is born evil. As other verses explicitly state, it is quite the opposite. We are all born as innocent inextricable parts of the Great Integrity, incapable of any corrupt act. We learn to be dishonest from a society that rewards deceit. Lao Tzu suggests that therefore don't reject any person, but rather cast away the opportunities to live selfishly. Then the Great Integrity will more and more permeate our lives, fulfilling our essential natures and needs.

Of course, such a premise is opposite to the doctrine that we are all born evil, inheriting the original sin of Adam and Eve. Had Lao Tzu known of Genesis, he might have proposed that the expulsion of Adam and Eve from the Garden of Eden was a metaphor, not about eating from the tree of knowing and reason, but about consuming the fruit of rationalization to justify the institutionalization of inequities among human beings. Lao Tzu argues that our solution to corruption and immorality is not to cast away human beings, but to cast away the system of temptations and opportunities to abuse others.

But the fundamentalists among us would say that Genesis is no metaphor. It is a literal historical account. Since belief cannot be a productive subject for debate, we might shift the discussion to a question of good humored and non-judgmental facetious levity: how in all these centuries of religious paintings has Eve always inherited a navel?

# Verse 63

## THE SECRETS OF GETTING THINGS DONE

Act without acting on.
Work without working at.

Enter bountifulness
when it is still insufficiency.
Answer with kindness
when faced with hostility.

Begin a difficult task in its easy stage
because large problems
grow from small ones.

Begin a large task in its formative state
because complex issues
originate from simple ones.

But beware of those
who promise quick and easy solutions!
Accept problems as challenges.

In this way,
the sage accomplishes great tasks
without ever
having to struggle with them.

## VERSE 63 COMMENTARY

Lao Tzu's secrets for getting things done are: 1) act without acting on, 2) work without working at, 3) begin at the early stages of a process, 4) answer hostility with kindness, and 5) avoid illusory easy solutions.

What he means by *acting without acting on*, *working without working at*, and *accomplishing without ever having to struggle* is to become part of processes in motion rather than to work against processes. *Acting on*, *working at*, and *struggling with* are all coercive activities, and Lao Tzu's most important advice in life is to avoid coercion. It is, of course, precisely opposite to how most of our institutions are programmed. Young people, for the most part, go to school because they are required to do so. Adults go to work because, if they don't, they will not receive the necessities of life. Most people go to church because they believe that if they don't go, they won't get into heaven. Most people don't commit crimes, because, if they do, they will go to prison. Even most babies and young children are accommodated to the system of coercion by physical punishment when they do something that displeases their parents. Lao Tzu says all this is wrong. The use of force indoctrinates us into behaving contrary to our human natures and contrary to the Great Integrity.

Line 3 in the extant Chinese version is omitted because it seems irrelevant to the rest of the verse and incomprehensible. It reads: "Taste without tasting".

# *Verse* 64

## TIMING

It is easy to hold what is still stable.
It is easy to mold what is not yet formed.
It is easy to shatter what is still fragile.
It is easy to scatter
what is yet light and small.
Therefore, act now rather than wait.
Get things done before it's too late.

A huge tree
that you can't get your arms around
grows from a tiny seedling birth.
A tower of nine stories high
rises from a small heap of earth.

A thousand mile journey
begins with one step.
This is an ancient tale.
Those who procrastinate,
or act prematurely, fail.

Those who interfere in processes
disrupt them.
Those who hold tightly to possessions
lose everything.
Wise people succeed
because they never force an outcome.
They never suffer a loss
because they are not attached to anything.

Some succeed in gathering assets.
But when the stakes begin to sail,
and greed crashes
through all cautionary boundaries,
failures unmercifully prevail.

Wise people don't accumulate possessions,
or teach anyone to amass things.
They devote themselves
to the natural rhythms
that the Great Integrity brings.

## VERSE 64 COMMENTARY

Timing for Lao Tzu is always a matter of becoming in tune with the natural rhythms of processes. To do so is to avoid all premature or procrastinated actions, as well as to avoid corrupting and disrupting these processes. As we would say in our modern colloquial vernacular – *Go with the flow*!

# Verse 65

## THE LOSS OF INNOCENCE

In ancient times,
before there were those
who were governed,
and those who governed over,
the sage blended with others,
and all was done
through the Primal Simplicity.
People lived in innocence.

When the Great Fragmentation
replaced the Great Integrity,
cleverness defeated wisdom.
Even some enlightened sages
became victims of the rulers
commanding the highest intrigue.

## VERSE 65 COMMENTARY

Two eras are contrasted: 1) *ancient times,* before there were castes and classes dividing human beings, and when tribal people *lived in innocence,* and 2) civilized times *when the Great Fragmentation replaced the Great Integrity,* and when the rulers and intellectuals traded wisdom for cleverness. In this second era, the over-privileged has utilized the *highest intrigue* to gain and sustain power over everyone else – even over some formerly enlightened sages.

# *Verse* 66

## WISDOM ALWAYS COMES FROM BELOW

Why do all the hundreds of great rivers
flow naturally to the sea?
Because the sea
is always lower than the rivers.

When are thousands of people
attracted to a sage?
When she positions herself below them,
always listening,
tirelessly responding to their needs.

Never commanding.
Never coercing.
Never manipulating.

Such a sage is forever adored.
Since she treats everyone
with love and respect,
everyone loves and respects her.

## VERSE 66 COMMENTARY

This is a simple ode to mutual love, respect, humility, devotion, responsiveness, and to always being there to listen to and care for each other. Such wisdom of behavior is such an antithesis to our all too common social relations, which are often characterized by *commanding, coercing* and *manipulating* each other.

# Verse 67

## THE THREE TREASURES

When most people hear
about the Great Integrity,
they say it is useless folly.
Because it is not like anything
in the world we know,
they also find it inconceivable.

On the contrary!
The Great Integrity has given us
three treasures to cherish:
The first is love.
The second is moderation.
The third is humility.

If you love,
you will be fearless.

If you are moderate,
you might always sense abundance in life.
If you live in humility,
you will be widely trusted.

But you will not have the capacity to love
if you are fearful.
Even worse, if you are fearless
and without love,
you will always be courting disaster.

If you live in insufficiency,
you have no opportunity to be moderate.
If you live in overabundance,
you not only live immoderately,
but are always courting disaster.

If no one trusts you,
then compensatory ego
will preclude humility.
If everyone trusts you,

and you lack humility,
you will always court disaster.

The three treasures
are practical guides to the Great Integrity.
The greatest foolishness
is to live without them.

## VERSE 67 COMMENTARY

The three treasures are both expressions of the Great Integrity as well as prerequisites for achieving it. They are also interrelated and inextricable from each other. In fact, it is not possible to fully achieve one without also achieving the other two.

*Love* is the primary treasure. It is the very heart of the Great Integrity. It is our ability to fully identify and empathize with the wondrous beings and entities of this remarkable universe. But love requires a combination of fearlessness and assertiveness along with caring and empathy. If we are fearful, our timidity blocks our freedom to express the love in our hearts. If we are fearless, but lack caring and empathy, then we always court disaster to ourselves and to all with whom we relate.

*Moderation*, like love, is a natural treasure of the Great Integrity. It is when competition and extreme mal-distributions of wealth replace cooperation and equitable divisions of the community's resources that moderation is sacrificed to greed and insufficiency. Those who live in insufficiency never have the opportunity to be moderate, and those who live in overabundance allow their greed to rob them of this treasure, thereby also courting disaster for themselves and others.

*Humility* is the third treasure. If our lives are governed by our egos, there is no space for humility. The excessive expression of our egos is a compensation for the starvation of our humanity and for our need to be appreciated, and also as a means to coerce others. Lao Tzu says if no one trusts us because of our inflated egos, we sacrifice ever being able to acquire this third treasure. However, if people do trust us, even if we fail to relate to others in humility, then we will bring on a third way of courting disaster.

Lao Tzu characterizes these three treasures as *practical guides to the Great Integrity*. He reminds us that living without them is the greatest foolishness because we thereby deny ourselves the very humanity that is essential to fulfill our lives.

# *Verse* 68

## THE ETHICS OF WAR

The best soldier fights
without vengeance,
without anger
and without hate.

He puts himself humbly
below his comrades,
thereby eliciting
the highest loyalty from them.

This is the power
of non-belligerence
and cooperation.
It is the ancient path to the Great Integrity.

## VERSE 68 COMMENTARY

As in so many verses, Lao Tzu focuses here on paradox. Soldiers are known for their vengefulness, anger, hate, arrogance and belligerence. His ideal soldier transcends these qualities because, in spite of his profession, he is on the ancient path to the Great Integrity.

Lao Tzu assumes that in "this period" when the Great Integrity is violated by all nations and civilizations, war is an on-going part of the "normal" misery of life. However, he differentiates between just and unjust acts of war. War is justified only to defend against acts of aggression, and even then only if committed without anger or hate.

There is a story that Ram Das tells about a famous Japanese samurai who was murdered by a violent criminal. The samurai's disciple vowed to rid the world of this evil man so that he could never murder anyone else. It took him years of searching before finally he found this criminal. The samurai drew his sword, and as he was about to fulfill his vow, the criminal spit in his face, which, of course, made him very angry. He placed his sword back in its scabbard and calmly left the room rather than kill someone in anger.

# Verse 69

## IN WAR THE DEFENDER WILL BE VICTORIOUS

There is a saying among those
wise in military affairs:
"We do not act as host
taking the initiative,
but would rather be the guest
assuming the defensive posture.
Rather than advancing one inch,
we prefer to retreat one foot."

This is called advancing without moving,
rolling up one's sleeves
without baring one's arms,
fighting without weapons,
capturing the enemy without attacking.

There is no greater disaster
than boasting of one's invincibility.
Such boasts lead to the loss
of the Three Treasures.
Therefore, when two opposing sides
meet in battle,
the one without an enemy
will be victorious.

## VERSE 69 COMMENTARY

Lao Tzu reasserts his position that the only justification for war is defense, and that those who defend themselves against aggression will ultimately be victorious. Those who are the arrogant aggressors will not only ultimately lose the war, but will also lose the Three Treasures of the Great Integrity. (See *Verse 67*.)

# Verse 70

## SO EASY TO UNDERSTAND AND PRACTICE!

The Great Integrity is easy to understand,
and easy to practice.
Yet it is not understood.
Nor is it practiced.

It is not understood
because people's heads are filled
with 10,000 trivia and rationalizations,
leaving no space for anything else.

It is not practiced
because people are busy, and bored,
with the 10,000 corruptions and miseries
that leave no time for the Three Treasures.

The Great Integrity is so ancient,
as old as the universe itself!
How can we expect people to remember it
after so many millennia of repression?

That is why
sages dress in rags
while they wear the Three Treasures
deep inside their hearts.

## VERSE 70 COMMENTARY

Lao Tzu points out here that the Great Integrity is not understood because our heads are filled with trivia and rationalizations, leaving no room for knowing the natural world.

It is not practiced because most of us are caught up in superficial and unfulfilling activities.

Lao Tzu also reminds us of a further difficulty in understanding and practicing the Great Integrity – *How can we expect people to remember it after so many millennia of repression?*

# Verse 71

## HEALING THE MIND

Academia confuses
knowledge with knowing.
Most everyone applauds
the memorization of the 10,000 trivia.
Beware!
These schooled addictions
are not just myths –
They are a form of mental illness.

Any fragment of the mind,
divorced from heart,
spirit, human community,
and from the primal reality
of the universe,
is an abomination
of the Great Integrity.

Let us prepare
for the Great Integrity
by cleansing ourselves
of all cobwebs
of cluttered fragments
that paralyze the mind.

In this way
we will function as our own holistic
physicians.

## VERSE 71 COMMENTARY

Although the main intent of this verse is kept intact, some liberties have been taken in the translation to clarify why Lao Tzu identifies the memorization of "facts", not only as violations of the Great Integrity, but as a form of mental illness. We need to be our own holistic physicians to heal our fragmentized minds so they can join our hearts, spirits, human communities and primal reality in the Great Integrity.

# Verse 72

## COMPARING COERCIVE POWER AND THE EMPOWERMENT OF THE GREAT INTEGRITY

When people no longer fear
the power of governments,
a far greater empowerment appears –
the Great Integrity –
which never needs to enforce itself.

Then, we will never again
be driven from our homes
or be compelled to labor
for the benefit of others.
We will all work naturally
to fulfill ourselves,
and to meet our community needs.

In the Great Integrity,
we will all love ourselves and all others,
not as compensations
for ego deprivations and defilements,
but as natural expressions
of our humanity.

## VERSE 72 COMMENTARY

Here, as in *Verse 71*, the translation follows the general intent of the verse while expressing it in more modern terms. Lao Tzu compares life as experienced through coercive power with life when all people are fully empowered by the Great Integrity, that is, the freedom to fully love and serve oneself and all others as natural expressions of our human natures.

Again and again Lao Tzu returns to the basic proposition that our coercive way of life is an unnatural violation of the Great Integrity and of our essential humanity. However, some day we'll live without coercion, celebrating each other *as natural expressions of our humanity*. The entire *Tao Te Ching* is an affirmation of this premise.

# *Verse* 73

## COURAGE, AND PATIENCE

The world we live in requires
great courage and patience.
Those with great courage,
but little patience,
tend to kill or be killed.
Those with great courage
as well as great patience
will tend to survive.
But the Great Integrity never judges you
for whatever path you happen to take.

The Great Integrity never strives
but always fulfills itself,
never is commanded but always responds,
never is summoned but always appears,
never is impatient but all is done on time.

## VERSE 73 COMMENTARY

In this verse, Lao Tzu looks at life from two points of view. In the first stanza he observes that because there is so much misery and conflict in the world, we must acquire great courage and patience to survive. When we acquire both courage and patience, we might survive, but, until we acquire the Great Integrity, the world will continue to generate misery and conflict. When we acquire great courage but lack patience, we endanger others and ourselves. He further observes that whichever of these survival mechanisms we use, the Great Integrity does not pass judgment upon us because each of us utilizes whatever defenses we have against the social condition we have inherited, and because blame and guilt are alien, and indeed toxic, to the Great Integrity.

In the second stanza, Lao Tzu observes the paradoxes of the world after we transform it. Then, living in the Great Integrity, we will fulfill ourselves naturally. We will respond without being commanded. We will appear without being coerced to be in any given place, and we will accomplish everything we need to do without being driven by that impatience which now originates in our being out of harmony with the very processes of which we are a part.

# *Verse* 74

## RULING BY FEAR

People do not fear death
when they are forced to live
in hopeless misery,
Thereby the executioners are no threat
to fearless rebels
who dare to make trouble.
They might even execute the executioners.

When people do fear death,
they do not defy the executioners at first.
But how long can the killings go on
before those who fear death
also become fearless?
Then, they too
might execute the executioners.

By that time, the only ones left
who might serve as the executioners
would be the people themselves.
However, it is said that those who hew wood
in place of skilled carpenters
are likely to cut their own hands.

## VERSE 74 COMMENTARY

The ultimate problem for those who rule by fear and force is created when their rule produces such misery and hopelessness that their victims no longer fear death because life itself becomes worse then death. Then, the people rise up and rid the world of the professionals who are paid to keep them in misery. When there are no longer professionals to keep the people victimized, then the rulers are forced to bribe some of the people themselves to do the dirty work. But Lao Tzu reminds us that this won't work so well because, not being professionals, they will be more likely to hurt themselves than their own family and friends.

# *Verse* 75

## WHO CAN ENJOY THE TREASURES OF LIFE?

Why are the people so hungry?
Because their grain is devoured
by the rich in taxes.
That is why the people are starving.

Why are the people so rebellious?
Because the government deprives them
of their liberties and rights.
That's why the people are rebellious.

Why do the people not fear death?
Because their lives
are made so miserable
that death seems no worse than life.

Thus, no one enjoys the treasures of life –
neither the rich
who squander their humanity,
nor the government,
which tyrannizes the people,
nor the people
who have nothing to gain from life.

## VERSE 75 COMMENTARY

The translation here follows the original very closely until the last stanza which I believe successive translators may have altered to mystify the entire point of the verse out of fear of the consequences of openly criticizing the power elite.

For example, Gregory C. Richter ( Red Mansions publ, 1998) provides a character-by-character translation of the last stanza as: "For those who do not use their life to act are able to value life."

Jonathan Star's version (Tarcher/Putnam, 2001) is: "In the end, the treasure of life is missed by those who hold on and gained by those who let go."

Clearly what this verse asks and answers is why people are starving, rebellious, and do not fear death. My departure from the last line of the extant Chinese text is to avoid its irrelevance to the rest of the Verse.

# *Verse* 76

## LET YIN PREDOMINATE

When we are born,
we are soft and supple.
But when we've perished
there's no more tenderness
to be cherished.

When plants are young,
they are pliant and fragile.
When they die,
as they lose their green,
they wither and dry.

The sharp sword and knife
tryst always with death,
while love without strife
is an ever devoted
disciple of life.

An inflexible army
seals its own fate.
When a tree branch grows brittle,
it easily snaps,
whether long or little.

Wherever you go,
the rigid lie low.
While the weightless in the sky,
and all that is gentle,
fly boundlessly high.

## VERSE 76 COMMENTARY

This verse, like *Verses 5, 42, 45* and *77*, elucidates the Chinese law of opposites: yin and yang, soft and hard, accepting and blaming, peace and war, harmony and antagonism.

The verse is a gentle metaphoric knock on the door of our consciousness, implying that hardness, inflexibility, war and coercion are not the nature of reality, but just the nature of our current social reality. Instead, we can make our lives peaceful, gentle, loving and flexible.

This verse also suggests that every extreme eventually turns into its opposite. Yin turns into yang and yang into yin. The entire evolution of species may be seen as five enormous evolutionary transformations: (1) From our yang origins of life in the sea as singled-cell amoeba-like creatures, to (2) the arising of yin plants always rooted somewhere, to (3) the transformation to complex yang sea fishes and then land animals, to (4) the development of more yin human beings living in communal clans and then tribes and more or less in harmony with nature, and (5) the birth of yang human beings in fiercely competitive groups, cities, states, countries, religions, ethnocentricities, ego-centricities, and all manners of hostilities and animosities.

If we are going to survive the extreme forms of violence that we have now coupled with extremely high developments of technology, we need to enter our next, and probably for us human beings, our final evolutionary transformation as a planetary totally cooperative species who once more harmonizes with nature, with each other and within ourselves. However our transformation to the *yin* Great Integrity will be on a conscious, and therefore much higher level than any form of life has ever experienced before.

The prophetic wisdom of Lao Tzu relentlessly focuses on the shift in dominance from yang to yin – aggressive to yielding, from hard to soft, from war to peace, from hating to loving, and from hostile aggressive nations to a Great Universal Integrity. How unbelievable that it has taken us all these twenty-seven centuries to make this theory (*Tao*) and practice (*Te*) our guide book (*Ching*) to the first evolutionary leap that has ever been possible to effectuate consciously. Thank you, Lao Tzu, for creating our *Guide to the Theory and Practice of the Great Integrity*! If we follow it, all future generations will honor you and us. However, if we fail to create an alternative humane consciousness, and the appropriate social, economic and cultural institutions to nurture our new incredible technologies, there might not be any generations of the future to honor either you or us.

# *Verse* 77

## TWO OPPOSITE PROCESSES

The Way of the Great Integrity
is like stringing a bow,
pulling down the high,
lifting up the low –

Shortening the long,
lengthening the short
to take from the excessive
and give insufficiency support.

How opposite to our social norms
which increasingly impoverish the poor
to further enrich the rich
who do not need any more.

How can we gather the world's wealth
to create abundance for all in need?
Through rediscovering the Great Integrity,
by acting without praising the deed.

## VERSE 77 COMMENTARY

The Great Integrity always balances yin and yang, diminishing the surplus (yang) to normalize the deficiency (yin).

The process of the marketplace is opposite – selfish beyond bounds – always forcing the poor to create more wealth for the wealthy.

As the last stanza implies, rediscovering the Great Integrity is the key to the transcendence of all the inhumanities of our ever-widening inequities.

# *Verse* 78

## APPEARANCE AND REALITY

Nothing in the world
is softer and weaker than water.
Yet there is nothing better
for subduing all
that is harder and stronger.

Everyone observes
how weak overcomes strong,
how gentleness overcomes rigidity.
Yet, this principle is seldom
put into conscious practice.

Though some may say it is useless
to accept responsibility
for the calamities and toxicities
of the world,
taking such responsibility

might put us on the road
to the Great Integrity.

Just remember that truth
often masquerades as falsity,
and falsity as truth.

## VERSE 78 COMMENTARY

There are three juxtaposed paradoxes here: 1) That water, which appears to be softer and weaker than anything else in the world, can subdue the hardest and strongest materials, like the huge rocks that the mountain stream disintegrates in its incessant flow. 2) That *gentleness overcomes rigidity, yet this principle is seldom put into conscious practice*. Most of us resort to using verbal or physical force when confronted with resistance to our desires and needs. 3) That even though the calamities and toxicities we are subjected to in our daily lives come largely from the social condition we inherit, and this condition might appear to be nothing we can do anything about, such an assumption may be false.

# *Verse* 79

## THE TOXICITY OF BLAME

Harboring a resentment
is sure to leave some resentment behind.
How can this be good?
It cannot.
Therefore, the wise
accept all responsibility.

Although those who hold the power
keep blaming and bleeding the people,
the violated Great Integrity blames no one.
Once achieving the Great Integrity,
we will all function with a pure heart.

## VERSE 79 COMMENTARY

和大怨必有餘怨安可以為善是以聖人執左
契而不責於人故有德司契無德司徹天道
無親常與善人

This verse is a continuation of the previous one, which also proposes that taking responsibility is an alternative to blame. Here the emphasis is on the toxic effects of harboring resentments. The verse also differentiates the present situation (applicable both for Lao Tzu's time and our own), in which injustice prevails, from the future when we will again experience the Great Integrity.

He also reminds us that as long as our social condition remains toxic, blaming those who blame and who take advantage of others, only adds to the toxicity. He dreams aloud of the future when, once achieving the Great Integrity, everyone will function with a pure heart, and no one will engage in blameful and shameful acts.

# *Verse* 80

## TRANSFORMING OUR LIVES

Let us fashion small states
with few inhabitants
who, without stress, can produce
more than they require,
who are so happy with their lives
that they have no thought
of migrating elsewhere –

Who inherit weapons and armor,
but no need to use them,
who return to honest forms
of communication,
and the simple enjoyments
of an ecological way of life.

Although these states
may be so close to each other

that they hear the barking
of each other's dogs
and the crowing of each other's cocks,
living contentedly, they will have no need
to invade each other's space.

## VERSE 80 COMMENTARY

Coming toward the end of his argument for the Great Integrity, Lao Tzu simply states his utopian dream for a transition world of small non-competing states which produce all their needs without stress, and whose inhabitants live so contentedly, they have no need or desire to migrate to or invade their neighbors.

Today, this dream can come to fruition, not by going back to small states, but by creating a planetary village using an ultimate production and communication technology that is guided by a highly evolved consciousness and spirituality, all of which were beyond the wildest dreams of Lao Tzu.

# *Verse* 81

## THE PARADOXES OF LIFE

Profound words are not clever.
Clever words are not profound.

Wise people are not quarrelsome.
Quarrelsome people are not wise.

Those who are intelligent
are not ideologues.
Those who are ideologues
are not intelligent.

The enlightened never hoard anything.
They share their possessions.

The more they give,
the greater their abundance.

The Great Integrity
is the physician of the universe
who heals without harming
and who acts without contention.

## VERSE 81 COMMENTARY

This last verse reminds us of the incompatibilities of profundity and cleverness, wisdom and quarrelsomeness, intelligence and ideology, enlightenment and hoarding. In the last stanza, Lao Tzu casts a final hopeful glance at a possible future when we (the physician of the universe) will heal ourselves.

For us today, this final verse is a primal summary of the *Tao Te Ching* as our wake-up call, reminding us that we can no longer survive by cleverness, war, ideological rationalizations, and with our gross inequities. Twenty-seven centuries after Lao Tzu, we have at last created the technological basis for the Great Integrity: a potential planetary economy and communications capability of producing and distributing whatever human beings need anywhere on earth. We have only to transform our completely anachronistic social relations and consciousness, and release our long repressed spirituality.

Instead, we live in the greatest and most idiotic paradox of all time: we are utilizing the very technologies that can liberate us to create the most monstrous weapons of mass destruction that now threaten to murder every one of us on the planet.

In the entire evolution, every species, except ours, has been programmed by its genetics to live in accordance with its own nature. It is only we human beings who have evolved as a promise. Since we live largely according to our social development rather than our genetic commands, we fulfill our species potentials only to the extent that our social development actualizes these latencies.

Lao Tzu's message to us is that we do not have to continue to live in contradiction to nature and to our human nature. We can live in accordance with the Great Integrity. For him, it was a remarkable insight and a utopian dream. For us, we have a choice – and not much time to make our decision – either we find our loving hearts, dreams and alternatives in Lao Tzu's Great Integrity or we will be the first species to become extinct through our own self-induced absurdity.